DevOps Bootcamp

A fast-paced guide to implement DevOps with ease

Mitesh Soni

BIRMINGHAM - MUMBAI

DevOps Bootcamp

First published: May 2017

Production reference: 1260517

Published by Packt Publishing Ltd.
Livery Place
35 Livery Street
Birmingham
B3 2PB, UK.
ISBN 978-1-78728-596-5

www.packtpub.com

Credits

Author
Mitesh Soni

Reviewer
Daniel Jonathan Valik

Commissioning Editor
Pratik Shah

Acquisition Editor
 Divya Poojari

Content Development Editor
Deepti Thore

Technical Editor
Sneha Hanchate

Copy Editor
Safis Editing

Project Coordinator
Shweta Birwatkar

Proofreader
Safis Editing

Indexer
Mariammal Chettiyar

Graphics
Tania Dutta

Production Coordinator
Melwyn Dsa

About the Author

Mitesh Soni is an avid learner with 10 years' experience in the IT industry. He is an SCJP, SCWCD, VCP, IBM Urbancode, and IBM Bluemix-certified professional. He loves DevOps and cloud computing, and he also has an interest in programming in Java. He finds design patterns fascinating. He believes "a picture is worth a thousand words."

He loves to play with kids, fiddle with his camera, and take photographs at Indroda Park. He is addicted to taking pictures without knowing many technical details. He lives in the capital of Mahatma Gandhi's home state.

Mitesh has authored the following books with Packt:

- *Implementing DevOps with Microsoft Azure*
- *DevOps for Web Developers [Video]*
- *DevOps for Web Development*
- *Jenkins Essentials*
- *Learning Chef*

"I've missed more than 9,000 shots in my career. I've lost almost 300 games. 26 times, I've been trusted to take the game-winning shot and missed. I've failed over and over and over again in my life. And that is why I succeed."—Michael Jordan.

I've always thanked a lot of people who have been instrumental in contributing to my life's journey up to now, but I guess it's time to really acknowledge that one person who has been with me as long as I can remember.

With this book, I would like to thank the one and only invisible yet omnipresent Almighty. We share a mutual love and hate relationship and I really value it. You were always there equally during my good and bad times and without you, I wouldn't have made it this far!

Last but not the least, I want to thank all who taught me how to love myself, first!

About the Reviewer

Daniel Jonathan Valik is an industry expert in cloud services, Platform as a Service, Unified Communications and Collaborations technologies. He also has a profound knowhow and expertise in other areas like IOT, DevOps, Automation and Software Pipeline management solutions, Microservices, Containerization, Virtualization, Cloud Native Applications, Artificial Intelligence, Hosted PBX and Cloud Telephony, WebRTC, Unified Messaging, Contact Center Solutions and Communications Enabled Business Process design.

Daniel has worked in several different disciplines like Product Marketing, Product Management, Program Management, Evangelist and Strategy Adviser in the industry and has lived and worked in different regions like Europe, South East Asia and the United States. He has a double master degree in Change- and Strategic Management and is an author of several technical and business related books about Cloud Services, Unified Communications, DevOps, Cloud Services and migration, AI and Game Development.

www.PacktPub.com

eBooks, discount offers, and more

Did you know that Packt offers eBook versions of every book published, with PDF and ePub files available? You can upgrade to the eBook version at www.PacktPub.com and as a print book customer, you are entitled to a discount on the eBook copy. Get in touch with us at customercare@packtpub.com for more details.

At www.PacktPub.com, you can also read a collection of free technical articles, sign up for a range of free newsletters and receive exclusive discounts and offers on Packt books and eBooks.

https://www2.packtpub.com/books/subscription/packtlib

Do you need instant solutions to your IT questions? PacktLib is Packt's online digital book library. Here, you can search, access, and read Packt's entire library of books.

Why subscribe?

- Fully searchable across every book published by Packt
- Copy and paste, print, and bookmark content
- On demand and accessible via a web browser

Customer Feedback

Thanks for purchasing this Packt book. At Packt, quality is at the heart of our editorial process. To help us improve, please leave us an honest review on this book's Amazon page at https://www.amazon.com/dp/1787285960.

If you'd like to join our team of regular reviewers, you can e-mail us at customerreviews@packtpub.com. We award our regular reviewers with free eBooks and videos in exchange for their valuable feedback. Help us be relentless in improving our products!

I would like to dedicate this book to lot of people who gave me a ray of hope amidst darkness. I would like to dedicate this book to Shreyansh (Shreyu – my sister Jigisha's baby boy) who showed me the power of innocence and smiles, Vinay Kher for his blessing, my parents who are always there silently praying for me, Simba (Priyanka Agashe) for supporting and encouraging me all the time and forcing me to believe in myself Indian Army and all brave soldiers in uniform for protecting us.

Table of Contents

Preface

DevOps is not a tool, technology, process, or framework; DevOps is a culture. Culture is an organization-specific thing and it evolves with a combination of people, processes, and tools for continuous improvement with continuous innovations.

The price of doing the same thing over and over again is far higher than the price of change. Change is no threat to an organization's culture. Using disruptive innovations only improves the culture. To improve is to change in the right direction, and to be perfect is to change often in the right direction by learning from the mistakes or experiences. And just for some fun... "Change is inevitable—even from a vending machine nowadays."

DevOps is not about reaching a destination and enjoying the beauty of it and ending the tour. It is a never-ending process of continuous improvement where we innovate things and plan to reach the same destination by enjoying the journey or process. This process may differ each time we improve and innovate, but our goal doesn't change! The goal is to achieve faster time to market with best utilization of resources in a cost-effective manner with the highest customer satisfaction.

This book emphasizes not only the technology but also different practices that the DevOps culture should include. DevOps is in its early stage. Deciding what not to do is very important, when, as an organization, we go in the direction of improvements and innovations. It is important to decide not to do manual work when it is repetitive.

In this book, we will cover all the key practices of DevOps, such as continuous integration, resource provisioning using containers and cloud computing – IaaS (Amazon EC2 and Microsoft Azure virtual machines), and PaaS (Azure App Service or Azure Web Apps and Amazon Elastic Beanstalk), continuous delivery, continuous testing, and continuous deployment; how to automate build integration and provision resources in the cloud environment; deploying a web application into Amazon Elastic Beanstalk, Microsoft Azure Web Apps/App Service Environments; application monitoring in AWS and Microsoft Azure Public Cloud; and load testing in VSTS and Apache JMeter.

The main objective is to manage the application life cycle. By automating repetitive manual processes, we standardize the management of the application life cycle and avoid errors. We also provide governance to application life cycle management by providing approval-based application deployment to different environments in Jenkins and VSTS, both with plugins or out-of-the-box features.

For continuous integration and continuous release (continuous delivery and continuous deployment), we have used Jenkins and Visual Studio Team Services (VSTS). The orchestration of end-to-end automation and approval-based workflows is managed by Jenkins and VSTS.

Progress is impossible without a change in mindset, and in order to change anything we need to visualize the change. In this book, we will try to focus on the cultural journey in the land of DevOps using people (development team, QA team, operations team, cloud team, build engineers, infrastructure team, and so on), processes (continuous integration, automated resource provisioning, continuous delivery, continuous testing, continuous deployment, continuous monitoring, continuous improvement, and continuous innovation), and tools (open source and the Microsoft stack).

The main reasons to showcase processes or practices using open source and the Microsoft stack is to cultivate the feeling that it is not about tools; it is about the mindset! We can perform almost the same operations using any automation tools.

What this book covers

Chapter 1, *DevOps Concepts and Assessment Framework*, contains details on how to get a quick understanding of DevOps from 10,000 feet and how to prepare for changing a culture. It provides the base on which to build the foundation of the DevOps concepts by discussing what our goals are, as well as getting buy-in from organization management.

Chapter 2, *Continuous Integration*, explains how to install a Jenkins continuous integration server and perform various tasks related to compilation, unit test execution, code analysis, and creating a package file. This chapter also covers continuous integration using the Microsoft stack. The goal here is to gain as much information as you can about continuous integration as it is a base for the rest of the automation.

Chapter 3, *Containers*, explains how to use containers for a development or QA environment for better resource utilization. It contains details on how to create a Tomcat container so that we can deploy the application in it.

Chapter 4, *Cloud Computing and Configuration Management*, focuses on creating and configuring the environment for application deployment in cloud. It will cover the use of the Infrastructure as a Service and configuration management tool, Chef, to create a platform so that we can deploy an application later in the book using automation.

Chapter 5, *Continuous Delivery*, explains how to deploy a web application when the platform is ready in different ways. This will involve platforms such as AWS and Microsoft Azure Iaas, and PaaS offerings such as AWS Elastic Beanstalk and Microsoft Azure App Services. We will also cover script-based deployment and Jenkins' plugin-based deployment.

Chapter 6, *Automated Testing (Functional and Load Testing)*, explains the various types of testing that can be carried out after deploying the application in non-production environments. It covers how to utilize automated testing techniques to enhance the quality of an application, such as functional testing and load testing using open source tools.

Chapter 7, *Orchestration — End-to-End Automation*, contains various ways to automate application life cycle management using orchestration. The build pipeline is utilized to orchestrate continuous integration, continuous delivery, and continuous testing. build and release definitions are configured in a way to form a pipeline, so end-to-end automation with proper approval-based mechanism is achieved.

Chapter 8, *Security and Monitoring*, speaks about security based on roles with only specific stakeholders, so they can manage configuration and builds. We will explore various tools to automate application life cycle management, monitoring, as well as notifications of the outcome based on success and failure, so the stakeholders can take the necessary steps to fix it.

What you need for this book

This book assumes that you are familiar with at least the Java programming language. Knowledge of core Java and JEE is essential if you want to gain better insights from this book. Having a strong understanding of the deployment of a web application in application servers such as Tomcat will help you to understand the flow quickly. However, we have quickly provided an overview of it. As the application development life cycle will cover a lot of tools in general, it is essential to have some knowledge of code repositories, as well as IDE tools such as Eclipse, and build tools such as Ant and Maven.

Knowledge of code analysis tools will make your job easier in configuration and integration; however, it is not vital to perform the exercises given in the book. Most of the configuration steps are mentioned clearly, step by step, and by providing screenshots for clear visualization.

You will be walked through the steps required to get familiar with Jenkins, VSTS, Microsoft Azure Web Apps, and AWS Elastic Beanstalk. For Microsoft Azure, you can use a 1-month trial access. VSTS also comes with a trial account with some restrictions. AWS also has 1-year trial period with specific limitations.

Who this book is for

The book is aimed at IT developers and operations, administrators who want to quickly learn and implement the DevOps culture in their organization. This book is specially aimed at developers, technical leads, testers, and operational professionals, who are the target readers and will want to jumpstart containers, the Chef configuration management tool, Microsoft Azure PaaS, and offerings such as app services and SQL database to host applications. Readers are aware of the issues faced by development and operations teams as they are stakeholders in the application life cycle management process. The reason to jumpstart Jenkins Automation Server, Microsoft Azure PaaS, and VSTS is to understand the importance of their contribution to continuous integration, automated test case execution, and continuous delivery for effective application life cycle management.

It is good to have some prior experience of continuous integration, cloud computing, continuous delivery, and continuous deployment. You may be a novice or be experienced with continuous integration tools such as Jenkins. This book covers continuous integration, cloud computing, continuous delivery, and continuous deployment for a sample Java Spring-based application. The main objective is to see end-to-end automation and implement it on the open source and Microsoft technology stack that can be extended further based on the understanding gained from this book.

Conventions

In this book, you will find a number of text styles that distinguish between different kinds of information. Here are some examples of these styles and an explanation of their meaning.

Code words in text, database table names, folder names, filenames, file extensions, pathnames, dummy URLs, user input, and Twitter handles are shown as follows: "Mount the downloaded `WebStorm-10*.dmg` disk image file as another disk in your system."

A block of code is set as follows:

```
html, body, #map {
    height: 100%;
    margin: 0;
    padding: 0
}
```

Any command-line input or output is written as follows:

```
$ mkdir css
$ cd css
```

New terms and **important words** are shown in bold. Words that you see on the screen, for example, in menus or dialog boxes, appear in the text like this: "The shortcuts in this book are based on the Mac OS X 10.5+ scheme."

Warnings or important notes appear in a box like this.

Tips and tricks appear like this.

For this book we have outlined the shortcuts for the Mac OX platform if you are using the Windows version you can find the relevant shortcuts on the WebStorm help page https://www.jetbrains.com/webstorm/help/keyboard-shortcuts-by-category.html.

Reader feedback

Feedback from our readers is always welcome. Let us know what you think about this book-what you liked or disliked. Reader feedback is important for us as it helps us develop titles that you will really get the most out of.

To send us general feedback, simply e-mail feedback@packtpub.com, and mention the book's title in the subject of your message.

If there is a topic that you have expertise in and you are interested in either writing or contributing to a book, see our author guide at www.packtpub.com/authors.

Customer support

Now that you are the proud owner of a Packt book, we have a number of things to help you to get the most from your purchase.

Downloading the example code

You can download the example code files for this book from your account at http://www.packtpub.com. If you purchased this book elsewhere, you can visit http://www.packtpub.com/support and register to have the files e-mailed directly to you.

You can download the code files by following these steps:

1. Log in or register to our website using your e-mail address and password.
2. Hover the mouse pointer on the **SUPPORT** tab at the top.
3. Click on **Code Downloads & Errata**.
4. Enter the name of the book in the **Search** box.
5. Select the book for which you're looking to download the code files.
6. Choose from the drop-down menu where you purchased this book from.
7. Click on **Code Download**.

Once the file is downloaded, please make sure that you unzip or extract the folder using the latest version of:

- WinRAR / 7-Zip for Windows
- Zipeg / iZip / UnRarX for Mac
- 7-Zip / PeaZip for Linux

The code bundle for the book is also hosted on GitHub at https://github.com/PacktPublishing/DevOps-Bootcamp. We also have other code bundles from our rich catalog of books and videos available at https://github.com/PacktPublishing/. Check them out!

Downloading the color images of this book

We also provide you with a PDF file that has color images of the screenshots/diagrams used in this book. The color images will help you better understand the changes in the output. You can download this file from `http://www.packtpub.com/sites/default/files/downloads/DevOpsBootcamp_ColorImages.pdf`.

Errata

Although we have taken every care to ensure the accuracy of our content, mistakes do happen. If you find a mistake in one of our books-maybe a mistake in the text or the code-we would be grateful if you could report this to us. By doing so, you can save other readers from frustration and help us improve subsequent versions of this book. If you find any errata, please report them by visiting `http://www.packtpub.com/submit-errata`, selecting your book, clicking on the **Errata Submission Form** link, and entering the details of your errata. Once your errata are verified, your submission will be accepted and the errata will be uploaded to our website or added to any list of existing errata under the Errata section of that title.

To view the previously submitted errata, go to `https://www.packtpub.com/books/content/support` and enter the name of the book in the search field. The required information will appear under the **Errata** section.

Piracy

Piracy of copyrighted material on the Internet is an ongoing problem across all media. At Packt, we take the protection of our copyright and licenses very seriously. If you come across any illegal copies of our works in any form on the Internet, please provide us with the location address or website name immediately so that we can pursue a remedy.

Please contact us at `copyright@packtpub.com` with a link to the suspected pirated material.

We appreciate your help in protecting our authors and our ability to bring you valuable content.

Questions

If you have a problem with any aspect of this book, you can contact us at `questions@packtpub.com`, and we will do our best to address the problem.

1
DevOps Concepts and Assessment Framework

Once you have an innovation culture, even those who are not scientists or engineers - poets, actors, journalists - they, as communities, embrace the meaning of what it is to be scientifically literate. They embrace the concept of an innovation culture. They vote in ways that promote it. They don't fight science and they don't fight technology

- Neil deGrasse Tyson

In this chapter, we will discuss how to quickly get an understanding of DevOps from 10,000 feet, with best practices on how to prepare for changing a culture. This will allow us to build the foundations of the DevOps concepts by discussing what our goals are, as well as getting buy-in from organization management. Basically, we will try to cover DevOps practices that can make application life cycle management easy and effective.

It is very important to understand that DevOps is not a framework, tool, or technology. It is more about the culture of an organization. It is also a way people work in an organization using defined processes and by utilizing automation tools to make daily work more effective and less manual.

To understand the basic importance of DevOps, we will cover the following topics in this chapter:

- Need for DevOps
- How DevOps culture can evolve
- Importance of PPT—people, process, and technology
- Why DevOps is not all about tools
- DevOps assessment questions

Need for DevOps

There is a famous quote by *Harriet Tubman* which you can find on (`http://harriettubmanb iography.com`). It says :

> *Every great dream begins with a dreamer. Always remember, you have within you the strength, the patience, and the passion to reach for the stars to change the world .*

Change is the law of life and that is applicable to organizations as well. If any organization or individual looks only at the past or present patterns, culture, or practices, then they are certain to miss future best practices. In the dynamic IT world, we need to keep pace with the technology evolution.

We can relate to *George Bernard Shaw*'s saying:

> *Progress is impossible without change, and those who cannot change their minds cannot change anything.*

Here, we are focusing on changing the way we manage the application life cycle.

The important question is whether we really need this change? Do we really need to go through the pain of this change?

The answer is yes.

One may say that such kinds of change in business or culture must not be forceful.

Agree.

Let's understand the pain points faced by organizations in application life cycle management in the modern world with the help of the following figure:

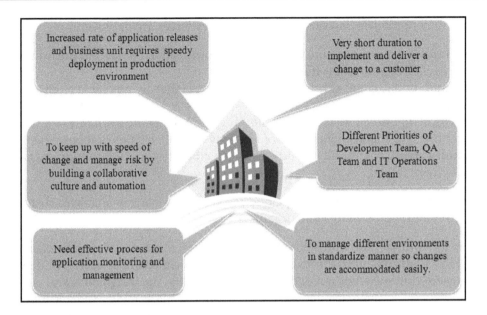

Considering the changing patterns and competitive environment in business, it is the need of the hour to improve application life cycle management.

Are there any factors that can be helpful in these modern times which can help us to improve application life cycle management?

Yes. Cloud computing has changed the game. It has opened doors for many path-breaking solutions and innovations. Let's understand what cloud computing really means and how terms like DevOps and automation play an important role for enterprise companies.

Overview of cloud computing

Cloud computing is the next logical step in terms of the evolution of computing. From traditional data centers and virtualization, to hybrid environments, private, public, and hybrid cloud services, cloud computing is a type of computing that provides multitenant or dedicated computing resources such as compute, storage, and network, which are delivered to cloud consumers on demand. It comes in different flavors which include **cloud deployment models** and **cloud service models**. The most important thing in this is the way its pricing model works, which is pay-as-you-go.

Cloud deployment models describe the way cloud resources are deployed:

1) **Private cloud**: private cloud consists of cloud resources that are behind the firewall and on-premise exclusively for a specific organization
2) **Public cloud:** public cloud consists of cloud resources that are available to all organizations and individuals
3) **Hybrid cloud**: hybrid cloud consists of cloud resources that are available to a specific set of organizations that share similar types of interests or similar types of requirements
4) **Community cloud**: community cloud consists of cloud resources that combine two or more deployment models

Cloud service models describe the way cloud resources are made available to customers of all kinds, from individuals and small organizations, to large enterprises.

It can be in the form of pure infrastructure, where virtual machines are accessible and controlled by cloud consumers or end users, that is, **Infrastructure as a Service (IaaS)**; or a platform where runtime environments are provided so that the installation and configuration of all software needed to run the application is already available and managed by cloud service providers, that is, **Platform as a service (PaaS)**; or **Software as a Service (SaaS)**, where the whole application is made available by cloud service providers with the responsibility of infrastructure and the platform remaining with the cloud service provider.

There are many **Service Models** that have emerged during the last few years, but **IaaS, PaaS**, and **SaaS** are based on the **National Institute of Standards and Technology (NIST)** definition:

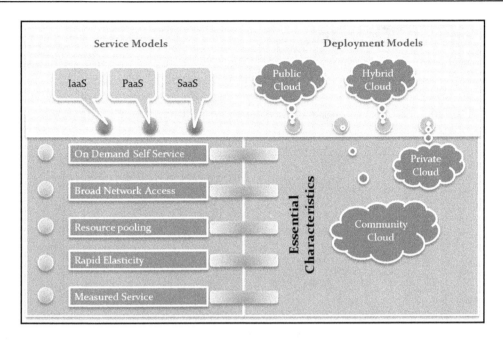

Cloud computing has a few characteristics that are significant such as multitenancy, pay-as-you-use similar to electricity or gas connection, **On Demand Self Service**, **Resource Pooling** for better utilization of compute, storage, and network resources, **Rapid Elasticity** for scaling up and scaling down resources, based on needs, in an automated fashion, and **Measured Service** for billing.

Over the years, the usage of different cloud deployment models has varied based on use cases. Initially, public cloud was used for applications that were considered noncritical, while private cloud was used for critical applications where security was a major concern.

Hybrid cloud and public cloud usage has evolved over time, with the experience and confidence in the services provided by cloud service providers. Similarly, the usage of different cloud service models has varied based on use cases and flexibility. IaaS was the most popular in the early days, but PaaS is catching up in its maturity and ease of use with enterprise capabilities such as auto-scaling, support for multiple programming languages, and support for end-to-end application life cycle management tools.

Overview of DevOps

DevOps is all about the culture of an organization, processes, and technology to develop communication and collaboration between development and IT operations teams to manage the application life cycle more effectively than the existing ways of doing it. We often tend to work based on patterns to find reusable solutions from similar kinds of problems or challenges.

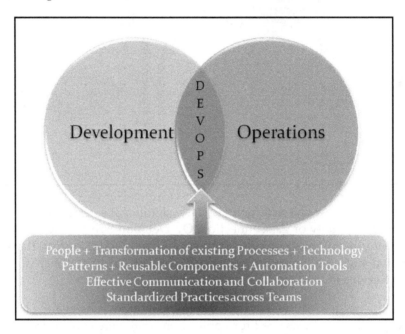

Over the years, achievements and failed experiments, best practices, automation scripts, configuration management tools, and methodologies have become an integral part of DevOps culture.

It helps to define practices for a way of designing, a way of developing, a way of testing, a way of setting up resources, a way of managing environments, a way of configuration management, a way of deploying an application, a way of gathering feedback, a way of code improvements, and a way of doing innovations.

The following are some of the visible benefits that can be achieved by implementing DevOps practices.

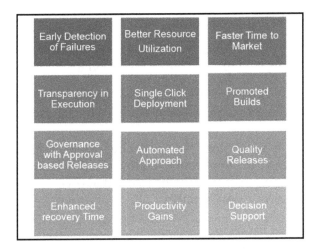

DevOps culture is considered an innovative package to integrate Dev and Ops teams in an effective manner that includes components such as continuous build integration, continuous testing, cloud resource provisioning, continuous delivery, continuous deployment, continuous monitoring, continuous feedback, continuous improvement, and continuous innovation to make application delivery faster, as per the demands of agile methodology. Evolving a culture is not an overnight journey. It takes a long time. However, there are also confusions regarding what DevOps is, hence, often only continuous integration or configuration management practices are considered as a DevOps practices implementation. It is a scenario similar to that of the elephant and five blind men, where every man touches a specific part of his body and assumes that to be an elephant.

However, it is not only the development and operations teams that are involved. The testing team, business analysts, build engineers, automation team, cloud team, and many other stakeholders are involved in this exercise of evolving the existing culture.

The DevOps culture is not much different than the organization culture, which has shared values and behavioral aspects. It needs adjustment in mindsets and processes to align with new technology and tools.

Challenges for the development and operations teams

There are some challenges, which is why this scenario has occurred and that is why DevOps is going in the upward direction and is the talk of the town in all information technology related discussions.

Challenges for the development team

Developers are enthusiastic and willing to adopt new technologies and approaches to solve problems. However, they face many challenges, including the following:

- The competitive market creates pressure for on-time delivery
- They have to take care of production-ready code management and new feature implementation
- The release cycle is often long, hence, the development team has to make assumptions before the application deployment finally takes place. In such a scenario, it takes more time to fix the issues that occur during deployment in the staging or production environment

Challenges for the operations team

The operations team is always careful in changing resources or using any new technologies or new approaches, as they want stability. However, they face many challenges, including the following:

- Resource contention: it's difficult to handle increasing resource demands
- Redesigning or tweaking: this is needed to run the application in the production environment
- Diagnosing and rectifying: they are supposed to diagnose and rectify issues after application deployment in isolation

Challenges for the IT team

The IT team provides resources to the respective teams to carry out the operations:

- Infrastructure provisioning: to provide infrastructure and a runtime environment with proper package installation on resources
- Configuration management: to upgrade the existing infrastructure or packages based on updates available in tools or technologies

Considering all the challenges faced by the development and operations teams, how should we improve existing processes, make use of automation tools to make processes more effective, and change people's mindset? Let's see in the next section on how to evolve the DevOps culture in an organization and improve efficiency and effectiveness.

How can DevOps culture evolve?

Inefficient estimation, a long time to market, and other issues led to a change in the waterfall model, resulting in the agile model. Evolving a culture is not a time-bound or overnight process. It can be a step-by-step and stagewise process that can be achieved without dependencies on the other stages.

We can achieve continuous integration without **Cloud Provisioning**. We can achieve **Cloud Provisioning** without **Configuration Management**. We can achieve **Continuous Testing** without any other DevOps practices. The following are different stages to achieve DevOps practices:

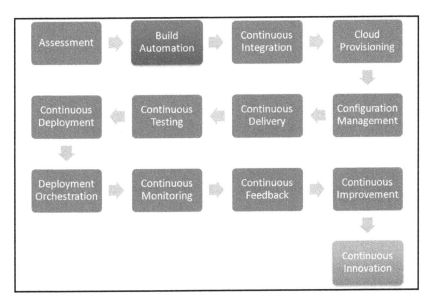

Agile development

Agile development or agile-based methodologies are useful for building an application by empowering individuals and encouraging interactions, giving importance to working software, customer collaboration—using feedback for improvement in subsequent steps—and responding to change in an efficient manner.

One of the most attractive benefits of agile development is continuous delivery in short time frames or, in agile terms, sprints. Thus, the agile approach of application development, improvement in technology, and disruptive innovations and approaches have created a gap between the development and operations teams.

DevOps

DevOps attempts to fill these gaps by developing a partnership between the development and operations teams. The DevOps movement emphasizes communication, collaboration, and integration between software developers and IT operations.

DevOps promotes collaboration, and collaboration is facilitated by automation and orchestration in order to improve processes. In other words, DevOps essentially extends the continuous development goals of the agile movement to continuous integration and release.

DevOps is a combination of agile practices and processes, leveraging the benefits of cloud solutions. Agile development and testing methodologies help us meet the goals of continuously integrating, developing, building, deploying, testing, and releasing applications.

Build automation

An automated build helps us create an application build using build automation tools such as Gradle, Apache Ant, and Apache Maven.

An automated build process includes activities such as compiling source code into class files or binary files, providing references to third-party library files, providing the path of configuration files, packaging class files or binary files into package files, executing automated test cases, deploying package files on local or remote machines, and reducing manual effort in creating the package file.

Continuous integration

In simple words, continuous integration or CI is a software engineering practice, where each check-in made by a developer is verified by either of the following:

- **Pull mechanism**: executing an automated build at a scheduled time
- **Push mechanism**: executing an automated build when changes are saved in the repository

This step is followed by executing a unit test against the latest changes available in the source code repository. Continuous integration is a popular DevOps practice that requires developers to integrate code into code repositories such as Git and SVN multiple times a day to verify the integrity of the code.

Each check-in is then verified by an automated build, allowing teams to detect problems early.

CI, and even CD, is the baseline for companies to even archive DevOps. We can't do DevOps without good CI and CD implementations in your organization.

Cloud provisioning

We have already covered the basics of cloud computing earlier in the chapter. Cloud provisioning has opened the door to treat **Infrastructure as Code (IAC)**, and that makes the entire process extremely efficient and effective, as we are automating a process which involved manual intervention to a huge extent.

The pay-as-you-go billing model has made the required resources more affordable to not only large organizations, but also to mid and small scale organizations, as well as individuals.

It helps to go for improvements and innovations, as earlier resource constraints were blocking organizations from going the extra mile because of cost and maintenance. Once we have agility in infrastructure resources, we can then think of automating the installation and configuration of packages that are required to run the application.

Configuration management

Configuration management (CM) manages changes in the system or, to be more specific, the server runtime environment. There are many tools available in the market with which we can achieve configuration management. The popular tools are Chef, Puppet, Ansible, Salt, and so on.

Let's consider an example where we need to manage multiple servers with the same kind of configuration.

For example, we need to install Tomcat on each server. What if we need to change the port on all servers, update some packages, or provide rights to some users? Any kind of modification in this scenario is a manual and, if so, error-prone process. As the same configuration is being used for all the servers, automation can be useful here.

Continuous delivery

Continuous delivery and continuous deployment are used interchangeably. However, there is a small difference between them.

Continuous delivery is process of deploying an application in any environment in an automated fashion and providing continuous feedback to improve its quality.

An automated approach may not change in continuous delivery and continuous deployment. The approval process and some other minor things can change.

Continuous testing and deployment

Continuous testing is the very important phase of the end-to-end application life cycle management process. It involves functional testing, performance testing, security testing, and so on.

Selenium, Appium, Apache JMeter, and many other tools can be utilized for the same.

Continuous deployment, on the other hand, is all about deploying an application with the latest changes to the production environment.

Continuous monitoring

Continuous monitoring is a backbone of the end-to-end delivery pipeline, and open source monitoring tools are like toppings on an ice cream scoop.

It is desirable to have monitoring at almost every stage in order to have transparency about all the processes, as shown in the following diagram. It also helps us troubleshoot quickly. Monitoring should be a well thought-out implementation of a plan.

Let's try to depict the entire process as a continuous approach in the following diagram:

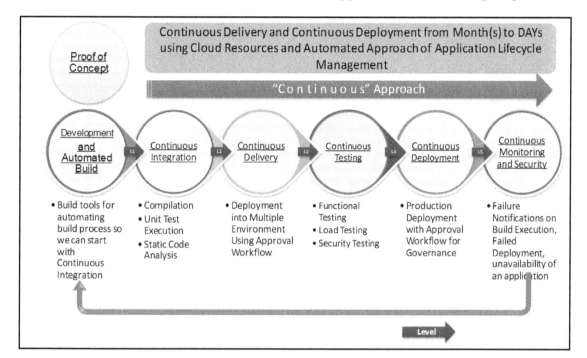

We need to understand here that it is a phased approach and it is not necessary to automate every phase of automation at once. It is more effective to take one DevOps practice at a time, implement it and realize its benefit before implementing another one.

This way we are safe enough to assess the improvements of changing the culture in the organization and remove manual efforts from the application life cycle management.

Importance of PPT - people, process, and technology

PPT is an important word in any organization. Wait! We are not talking about Powerpoint Presentation. Here, we are focusing on people, processes, and tools/technology. Let's understand why and how they are important in changing the culture of any organization.

People

As per the famous quote from Jack Canfield :

> *Successful people maintain a positive focus in life no matter what is going on around them. They stay focused on their past successes rather than their past failures, and on the next action steps they need to take to get them closer to the fulfillment of their goals rather than all the other distractions that life presents to them.*

A curious question could be, why do people matter? If we try to answer this in one sentence, then it would be: Because we are trying to change culture.

So?

People are an important part of any culture and only people can drive the change or change themselves to adapt to new processes or define new processes and learn new tools or technologies.

Let's understand how and why with the *Formula for Change*.

David Gleicher created the *Formula for Change* in the early 1960s, as per references available in Wikipedia. Kathie Dannemiller refined it in 1980. This formula provides a model to assess the relative strengths affecting the possible success of organizational change initiatives.

Gleicher (original) version: *C = (ABD) > X, where: C = change, A = the status quo dissatisfaction, B = a desired clear state, D = is practical steps to the desired state, X = the cost of the change.*

Dannemiller version: *D x V x F > R; where D, V, and F must be present for organizational change to take place where: D = Dissatisfaction with how things are now, V = Vision of what is possible, F = First concrete steps that can be taken toward the vision. If the product of these three factors is greater than R = Resistance, then change is possible.*

Essentially, it implies that there has to be strong dissatisfaction with existing things or processes, vision of what is possible with new trends, technologies, and innovations with respect to the market scenario; concrete steps that can be taken toward achieving the vision.

 For more details on *Formula for Change*, you can visit this wiki page: `https ://en.wikipedia.org/wiki/Formula_for_change#cite_note-myth-1`

If it comes to sharing an experience, I would say it is very important to train people to adopt a new culture. It is a game of patience. We can't change the mindset of people overnight and we need to understand first before changing the culture.

Often, it is observed in the industry, that job opening with a DevOps knowledge or DevOps engineers, but ideally they should not be imported and people should instead be trained in the existing environment by changing things gradually to manage resistance. We don't need a special DevOps team; we need more communication and collaboration between developers, test teams, automation enablers, and the cloud or infrastructure team.

It is essential for all to understand the pain points of each other. In the organizations I have worked, we used to have a **Center of Excellence** (**COE**) in place to manage new technologies, innovations, or culture. As an automation enabler and part of the DevOps team, we should be working as a facilitator only and not a part of the silo.

Processes

Here is a famous quote from *Tom Peters*, which says:

> *Almost all quality improvement comes via simplification of design, manufacturing...*
> *layout, processes, and procedures*

Quality is extremely important when we are dealing with evolving a culture. We need processes and policies for doing things in a proper way and standardized across the projects so the sequence of operations, constraints, rules and so on are well defined to measure success.

We need to set processes for the following things:

- Agile planning
- Resource planning and provisioning
- Configuration management
- Role-based access control to cloud resources and other tools used in automation
- Static code analysis – rules for programming languages
- Testing methodology and tools
- Release management

These processes are also important for measuring success in the process of evolving DevOps culture.

Technology

Here is a famous quote from *Steve Jobs*, which says:

> *Technology is nothing. What's important is that you have a faith in people, that they're basically good and smart, and if you give them tools, they'll do wonderful things with them.*

Technology helps people and organizations to bring creativity and innovations while changing the culture. Without technology, it is difficult to achieve speed and effectiveness in the daily and routine automation operations. Cloud computing, configuration management tools, and the build pipeline are among a few that are useful in resource provisioning, installing a runtime environment, and orchestration. Essentially, it helps to speed up different aspects of application life cycle management.

Why DevOps is not all about tools

Yes, tools are nothing. They are not that important a factor in changing the culture of any organization. The reason is very simple. No matter what technology we use, we will perform continuous integration, cloud provisioning, configuration management, continuous delivery, continuous deployment, continuous monitoring, and so on.

Categorywise, different tool sets can be used, but all perform similar operations. It is just the way that tool performs a certain operation that differs, else the outcome is the same. The following are some of the tools based on the categories:

Category	Tools
Build automation	Nant, MSBuild, Maven, Ant and Gradle
Repository	Git and SVN
Static code analysis	Sonar and PMD
Continuous integration	Jenkins, Atlassian Bamboo, and VSTS
Configuration management	Chef, Puppet, Ansible, and Salt
Cloud platforms	AWS and Microsoft Azure
Cloud management tool	RightScale
Application deployment	Shell Scripts and Plugins
Functional testing	Selenium and Appium

Load testing	Apache Jmeter
Repositories	Artifactory, Nexus, and Fabric

Let's see how different tools can be useful in different stages for different operations. This may change based on the number of environments or the number of DevOps practices we follow in different organizations:

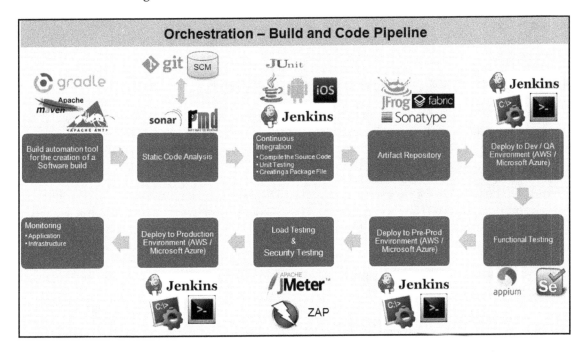

If we need to categorize tools based on different DevOps best practices, then we can categorize them based on open source and commercial categories. The following are just some examples:

Components	Open Source	IBM Urban Code	Electric-Cloud
Build tools	Ant or Maven or MS Build	Ant or Maven or MS Build	Ant or Maven or MS Build
Code repositories	Git or Subversion	Git or Atlassian Stash or Subversion or StarTeam	Git or Subversion or StarTeam
Code analysis tools	Sonar	Sonar	Sonar

Continuous integration	Jenkins	Jenkins or Atlassian Bamboo	Jenkins or ElectricAccelerator
Continuous delivery	Chef	Artifactory and IBM UrbanCode Deploy	ElectricFlow

In this book, we will try to focus on the open source category, as well as commercial tools. We will use Jenkins and Visual Studio Team Services for all the major automation and orchestration-related activities.

DevOps assessment questions

DevOps is a culture and we are very much aware of that fact. However, before implementing automation, putting processes in place and evolving culture, we need to understand the existing status of the organization's culture and whether we need to introduce new processes or automation tools.

We need to be very clear that we need to make the existing culture more efficient rather than importing culture. To accommodate an assessment framework is difficult, but we will try to provide some questions and hints based on which it will be easier to create an assessment framework.

Create categories for which we want to ask questions and get responses for specific applications.

The following are a few sample questions:

1. Do you follow agile principles?
2. Are you using any source code repository?
3. Are you using any tools for static code analysis?
4. Are you using any build automation tools?
5. Are you using on-premise infrastructure or cloud-based infrastructure?
6. Are you using any configuration management tools or scripts for installing application packages or a runtime environment?
7. Are you using any automated scripts to deploy applications in prod and nonprod environments?
8. Are you using any orchestration tools or scripts for application life cycle management?

9. Are you using automation tools for functional testing, load testing, security testing, and mobile testing?
10. Are you using any tools for application and infrastructure monitoring?

Once the questions are ready, prepare responses and, based on those responses, decide a rating for each response given for the preceding questions.

Make a framework flexible so, even if we change a question in any category, it will be managed automatically.

Once the rating is given, capture responses and calculate overall ratings by introducing different conditions and intelligence into the framework.

Create categorywise final ratings and create different kinds of charts from the final rating to improve the reading value of it. The important thing to note here is the significance of organizations' expertise in each area of application life cycle management. It will give the assessment framework a new dimension to add intelligence and make it more effective.

Summary

In this chapter, we have set many goals to achieve throughout this book. We have covered continuous integration, resource provisioning in the cloud environment, configuration management, continuous delivery, continuous deployment, and continuous monitoring.

Setting goals is the first step in turning the invisible into the visible.

-Tony Robbins

We have seen how cloud computing has changed the way innovation was previously perceived and how feasible it has become now. We have also covered the need for DevOps and all different DevOps practices in brief. People, processes, and technology are also important in this whole process of changing the existing culture of an organization. We tried to touch upon the reasons why they are important. Tools are important but not the show stopper; any toolset can be utilized and changing a culture doesn't need a specific set of tools. We have discussed in brief the DevOps assessment framework as well. It will help you to get going on the path of changing culture.

Faith is taking the first step even when you don't see the whole staircase.

-Martin Luther King, Jr.

In the next chapter, we will take our first step of this journey towards continuous integration. We will use Jenkins and Microsoft Visual Studio Team Services for implementing continuous integration and verify how CI can be implemented in different tools without any major challenges.

2
Continuous Integration

Continuous effort - not strength or intelligence - is the key to unlocking our potential
- Winston Churchill

In this chapter, we will cover how to install the continuous integration server Jenkins and perform various tasks related to compilation, unit test execution, code analysis, and creating a package file. We will also cover continuous integration using Microsoft stack. The goal here is to gain as much information as you can about the continuous integration as it is a base for the rest of the automation. Here is the gist of topics that we will cover:

- Installing Jenkins 2
- Configuring Maven-based JEE web application
- Integrating Jenkins and SonarQube
- Executing command-line operations from Jenkins
- Continuous integration using VSTS

Let's start with making ourselves aware about Jenkins—continuous integration server or automation server nowadays after Jenkins 2.0.

Installing Jenkins 2

Here are a few steps that we can follow to install Jenkins :

1. Install Java Development Kit 8 and set `JAVA_HOME` as the environment variable. In the Command Prompt or Terminal, verify that Java is installed properly or not by executing the `java -version`, `javac`, and `java` commands. Download `jenkins.war` from the Jenkins website.

2. To run Jenkins, execute `java -jar jenkins.war`. Wait until Jenkins is fully up and running.

3. Once Jenkins is fully up and running, open the browser and visit `http://<localhost/IP_ADDRESS>:8080`.

4. We need to unlock Jenkins first to go ahead with the configuration. Copy the password from the given file location or copy it from the console/terminal from where we executed the Java command.

5. Enter the **Administrator** password and click on **Continue**.

6. Install the suggested plugins or select plugins to install.

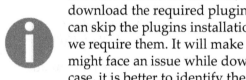 If we are behind the firewall, then it will ask for **Proxy Settings** so we can download the required plugins. If we are familiar with Jenkins, then we can skip the plugins installation completely and install them later on when we require them. It will make this configuration fast. Behind the proxy, we might face an issue while downloading some of the plugins. In such a case, it is better to identify these plugins and use **Select plugins** to **Install** option to avoid endless waiting or configuration failure.

7. Once we finish the plugins installation process or skip it, we need to create our first admin user. After Jenkins 2, plugin installation and security configuration are part of the initial setup and that is a step forward towards a matured tool.

8. Provide the required user details and click on **Save** and **Finish**. Now, Jenkins is ready and the Jenkins set up is complete. We can start using Jenkins. This is the time where we meet the Jenkins dashboard for the first time.

We can manage Jenkins-related configurations such as tools configurations, security configurations, creating build jobs, managing plugins, and managing agents.

The following screenshot represents the **Jenkins** dashboard:

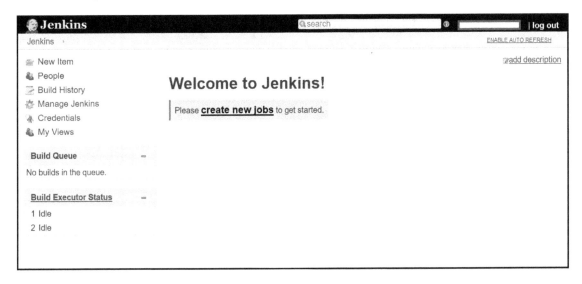

We will use the Java/JEE sample application in our automation objective. First of all, we need to inform Jenkins where our installable files are as they are required to execute certain tasks. As the Maven build tool is used in this application, we need a Maven installable folder too. Download Apache Maven. Go to **Manage Jenkins** in the Jenkins dashboard and click on **Global Tool Configuration**. Click on **Add JDK**. We have JDK installed already, so we can give the path of JAVA_HOME and our Java is configured properly.

Global Tool Configuration in Jenkins

In this section, we will configure various tools that we need to utilize at the time of creating a build job, for example, Java, Ant, Maven, and so on.

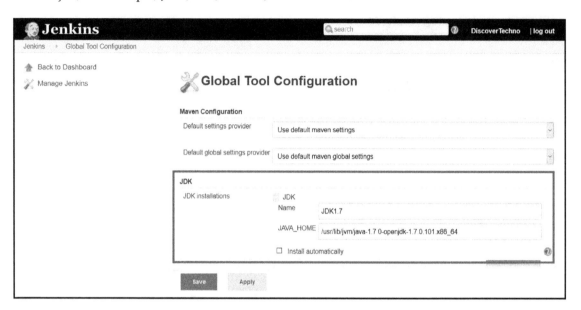

We can install this also from the **Jenkins** dashboard. What if we have two different applications where one needs to be compiled with JDK 1.7 and the other with JDK 1.8? We can add multiple JDK and while creating a **Build Job**, we can specify which JDK we want to utilize for that build job execution.

Once Java is configured, our next task is to configure **Maven**:

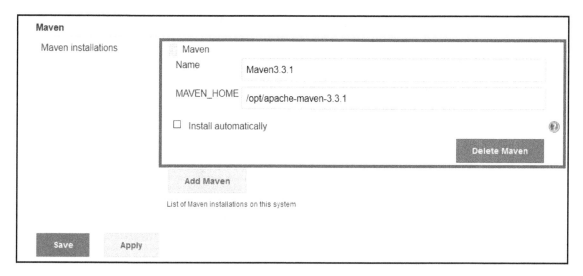

Now that we have configured different tools in Jenkins, we will create a new job or item using the **Jenkins** dashboard, so we can configure continuous integration for JEE-based applications.

Creating and configuring Maven-based JEE web applications

In this section, we will create a Maven-based Jenkins build job that will execute the pom.xml file for compilation, ubit test execution, and creating a package file. So let's begin!

On the **Jenkins** dashboard, click on **New Item**:

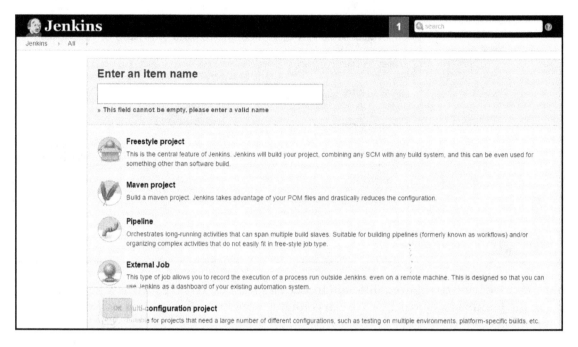

As it is a Maven-based project, we will select the **Maven project** template. In case it is an Ant-based application or any other automation task, then we can select the **Freestyle project** template to create **Build Job**. Select **Maven project** and click on **OK**. It will open the build job configuration page, as shown in the following screenshot:

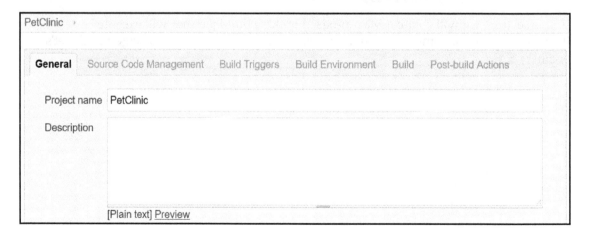

In **Source Code Management**, provide a GitHub URL, SVN URL (install the subversion plugin first), or any repository URL. We can also access the code available on the filesystem:

In the **Build** section, select the **Maven Version** that we have configured in the **Global Tool Configuration** section. Provide the Maven goal to be executed on pom.xml. For more details on Maven goals, go to the Apache Maven website. The **package** goal will compile the source code, execute the unit test case, and create a package or war file in the context of Java:

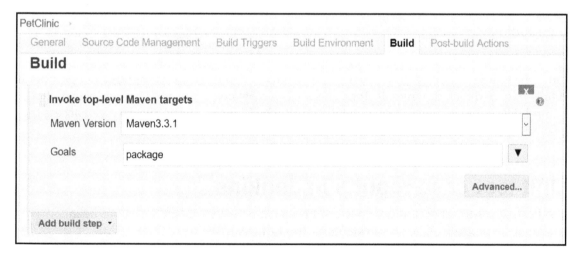

Click on **Apply** and **Save** on the job configuration page. Click on the **Build Now** link on the dashboard. Verify the **Build History** on the same page. The first build will be in progress.

Click on the progress bar to go to the console output directly on the **Jenkins** dashboard.

It will start fetching the code from the repository and put it into the local workspace. If it fetches the code successfully, then on a **Project** dashboard or on a **Build** dashboard, check **workspace**.

Wait until the **package** goal of Maven is executed in Jenkins. It will compile all source files, execute unit test cases written in JUnit, and create a WAR file that needs to be deployed in the web server such as Tomcat or JBoss:

```
Jenkins   PetClinic   #1

                      [INFO]
                      [INFO] --- maven-war-plugin:2.3:war (default-war) @ spring-petclinic ---
                      [INFO] Packaging webapp
                      [INFO] Assembling webapp [spring-petclinic] in [/home/mitesh/.jenkins/workspace
                      /PetClinic/target/spring-petclinic-4.2.5-SNAPSHOT]
                      [INFO] Processing war project
                      [INFO] Copying webapp resources [/home/mitesh/.jenkins/workspace/PetClinic
                      /src/main/webapp]
                      [INFO] Webapp assembled in [12697 msecs]
                      [INFO] Building war: /home/mitesh/.jenkins/workspace/PetClinic/target
                      /petclinic.war
                      [INFO] ------------------------------------------------------------------------
                      [INFO] BUILD SUCCESS
                      [INFO] ------------------------------------------------------------------------
                      [INFO] Total time: 03:14 min
                      [INFO] Finished at: 2016-04-27T12:15:29-07:00
                      [INFO] Final Memory: 27M/214M
                      [INFO] ------------------------------------------------------------------------
                      Finished: SUCCESS
```

Once the build is successful, our first target is achieved and that is continuous integration. If it fails due to Maven downloads, then check Maven-related settings. If Jenkins is installed behind the proxy, then give proxy details in Apache Maven's config file, so it can access the Maven repository and download the required files.

Unit test case results in Jenkins

To check the unit test execution, go to the **Project** and verify the build that has been executed successfully. Click on **Test Result (no failures)**:

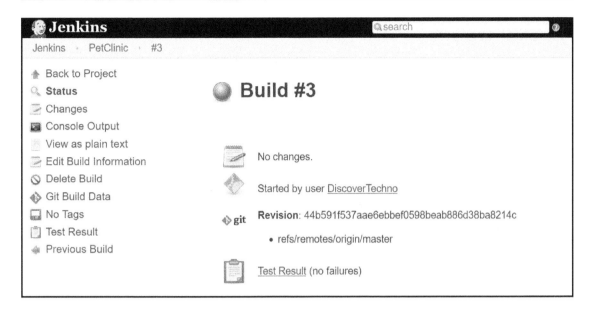

It will give a list of **Test Result** based on packages. To get more details, go to specific packages and verify the results:

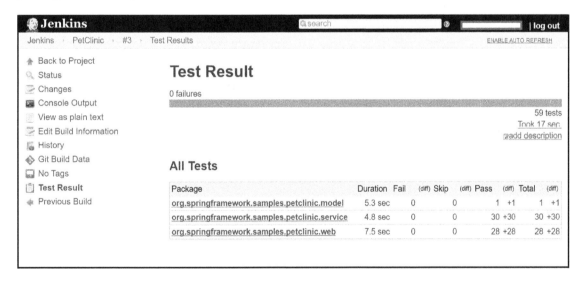

Master agent architecture in Jenkins

Let's consider a scenario where we have specific tools, which are on a different server and these tools are part of an important phase of application life cycle management.

In that case, we can use our Jenkins server as a master and the server with specific tools as the agent. In this way, master Jenkins can access resources available on other servers to execute specific operations.

Go to **Manage Jenkins** and click on **Manage Nodes**. We can see the **master** node available on which our Jenkins is installed. To add a new node that might have a different operating system and tool set, we need to click on **New Node**:

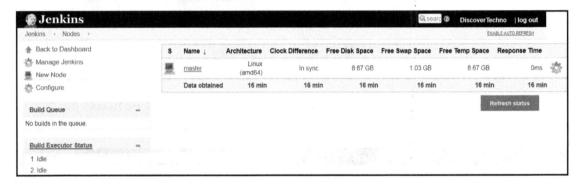

Give a node name and select it as a **Permanent Agent**. Click on **OK**. Enter **Name**, **Labels**, and **Remote root directory**. **Remote root directory** is the directory where all details of execution on the agent will be stored. It is similar to the JENKINS_HOME's workspace directory on the agent node:

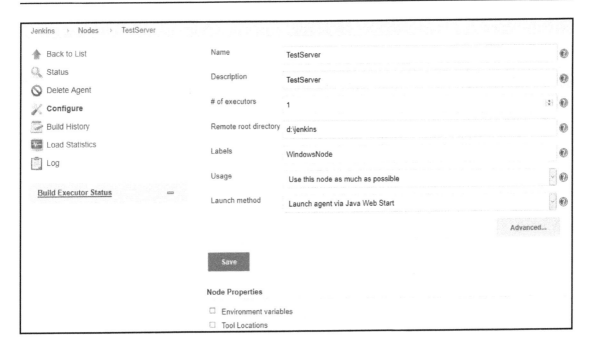

Click on **Save**; go to **Security Configuration** and **Enable Slave Agent Port** – TCP port for JNLP agents (keep it as random and not the disable state):

Go to the Agent configuration in Master Jenkins. Copy the command to **Run from agent command line**:

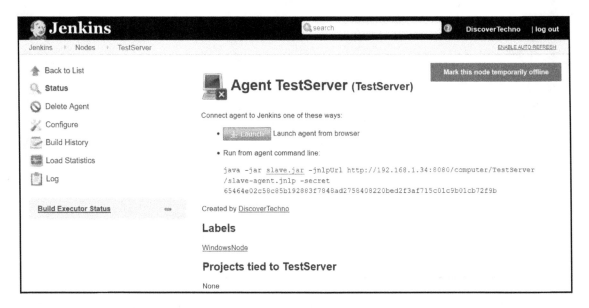

Download the `slave.jar` as well on the agent machine and execute the command as shown in the following screenshot:

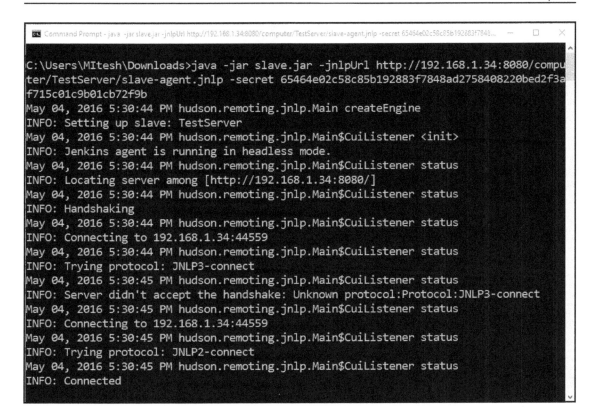

Once the agent is connected in the console, verify the same in **master** Jenkins as well:

S	Name ↓	Architecture	Clock Difference	Free Disk Space	Free Swap Space	Free Temp Space	Response Time	
	master	Linux (amd64)	In sync	8.60 GB	1.92 GB	8.60 GB	0ms	
	TestServer	Windows 8 (amd64)	In sync	N/A	3.56 GB	133.27 GB	2562ms	
	Data obtained	8 min 25 sec	8 min 25 sec	8 min 25 sec	8 min 22 sec	8 min 25 sec	8 min 25 sec	

Once we have the agent connected to the master, we can assign build jobs to be assigned to that agent for execution. Before executing build jobs on the agent, we need to make sure that all tools that are needed for execution are configured in master Jenkins as well so that master can use these installable for execution.

In the job configuration, we can select the **Restrict where this project can be run** checkbox and provide **Label Expression** for agent:

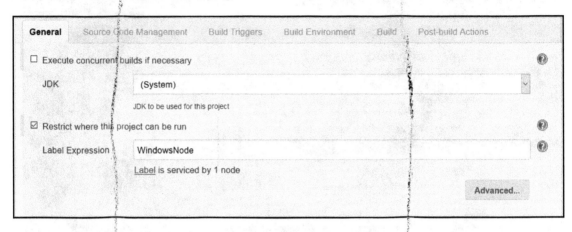

In the agent **Node** page, we can provide **Tool Locations**:

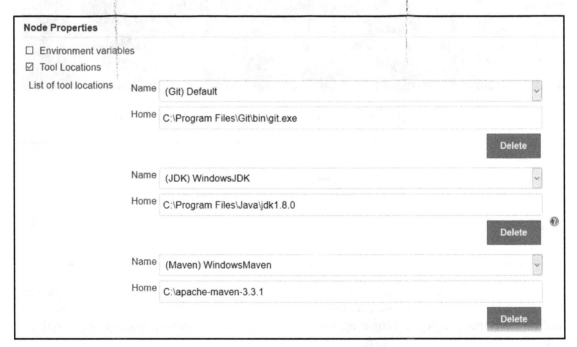

We can use such agents for static code analysis or test execution where different tools can be installed on agents and then agents are assigned to execute a job. Let's cover SonarQube in the next section.

Integrating Jenkins and SonarQube

So, first let's see how to configure SonarQube with Jenkins so that we can perform static code analysis by triggering it from Jenkins.

Go to **Manage Jenkins**, click on **Manage Plugins**, and then click on the **Available** tab. Find the SonarQube plugin and install it.

Go to **Manage Jenkins**, and then click on **Configure System**. Find the **SonarQube servers** section and click on the **Add SonarQube** server. Provide **Server URL** and credentials. Get a **Server authentication token** from SonarQube (Administration | Security | Users) and provide it in Jenkins:

Jenkins ▸ configuration		
SonarQube servers		
Environment variables	☐ Enable injection of SonarQube server configuration as build environment variables	
	If checked, job administrators will be able to inject a SonarQube server configuration as environment variables in the build.	
SonarQube installations	Name	Sonar
	Server URL	http://localhost:9000/
		Default is http://localhost:9000
	Server version	5.3 or higher ▾
		Configuration fields depend on the SonarQube server version.
	Server authentication token	••
		SonarQube authentication token. Mandatory when anonymous access is disabled.
	SonarQube account login	
		SonarQube account used to perform analysis. Mandatory when anonymous access is disabled. No longer used since SonarQube 5.3.
	SonarQube account password	
		SonarQube account used to perform analysis. Mandatory when anonymous access is disabled. No longer used since SonarQube 5.3.

Go to **Global Tool Configuration** in **Manage Jenkins** and configure the **SonarQube Scanner** to install automatically:

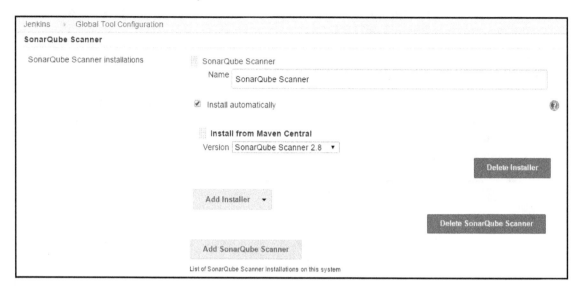

Create a new freestyle job in Jenkins. Configure JDK path of agent where SonarQube is installed.

Install the `Quality gate` plugin as well. By configuring the `Quality gate` plugin, we can fail the Jenkins build job if SonarQube analysis fails.

Configure the repository URL of the project. Go to Job configuration and in the **Build** step add **Execute SonarQube Scanner**. Select **JDK** and enter the path to `sonar-project.properties` or provide **Analysis properties**:

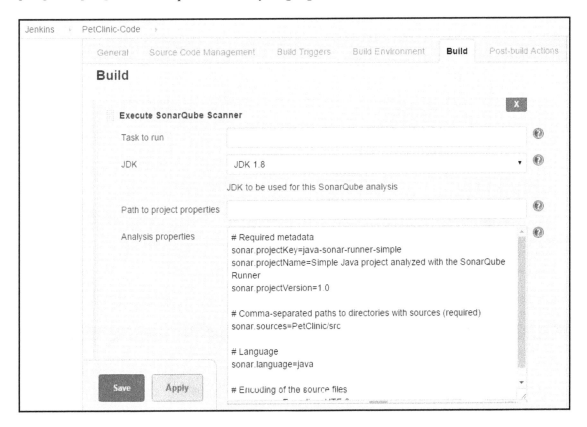

In **Post-build Actions**, select **Quality Gates**.

Enter the **Project Key** that we have given in analysis properties or `sonar-project.properties`:

Click on **Build now** and verify the results of build execution in Jenkins.

Go to the SonarQube server, and verify code analysis available in the **Dashboard**:

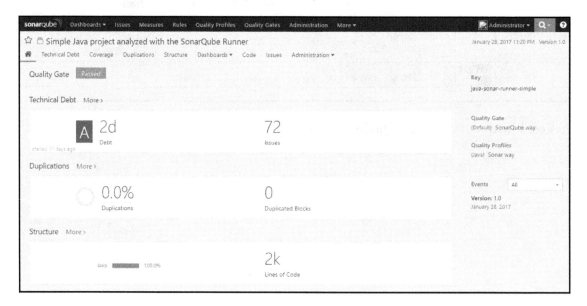

This is how we can integrate SonarQube in Jenkins. Let's see how we can send e-mail notifications from Jenkins.

E-mail notifications in Jenkins

Let's see how to configure e-mail notifications to send the status of job executions to specific stakeholders. Go to **Manage Jenkins**, click on **Configure System**, and configure the e-mail settings as shown in the following screenshot:

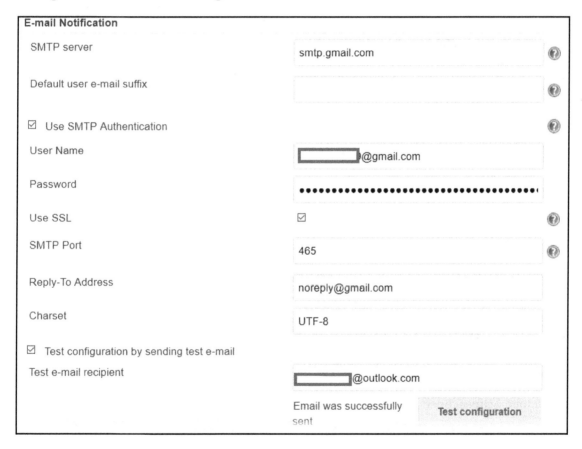

In the **Post-build Actions**, select **E-mail Notification** and configure **Recipients**. Save it:

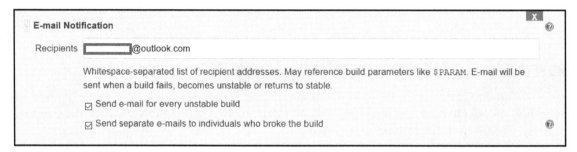

We can send a notification if it is an unstable build and we can send an e-mail to the individual who has broken the build.

In the next section, we will see how continuous integration can be performed using **Visual Studio Team Services** (**VSTS**).

Continuous integration using Visual Studio Team Services

We often say DevOps has nothing to do with the tools. All tools perform the same operation with some minor variations or flexibility. We will see how continuous integration can be performed using VSTS.

Create an **Account** in VSTS and create one **Project** with the name PetClinic.

Eclipse and VSTS integration

In this section, we will see how to integrate Eclipse and VSTS so we can commit the code from the local system to VSTS.

Download Eclipse, open it, and click on the **Help** menu. Select **Install New Software**.

Add a site to install the TFS plugin in Eclipse so we can commit code to VSTS from the Eclipse directly.

Select **Team Explorer Everywhere** and click on **Next**:

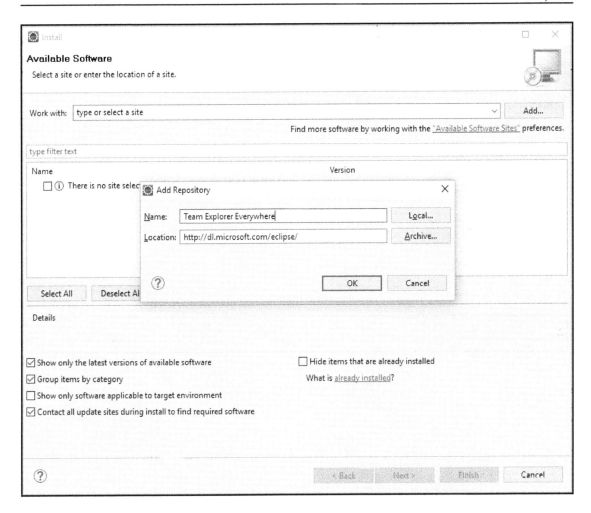

Review **Install Details** and click on **Next**.

Review **Licenses** and **Accept Terms** and click on **Finish**.

Wait until the installation is complete and restart the Eclipse.

In Eclipse, go to **Window** | **Perspective** | **Open Perspective** | **Other...** | **Select Team Foundation Server Exploring**.

Click on **Connect to Team Services or a Team Foundation Server**. We will connect with team services:

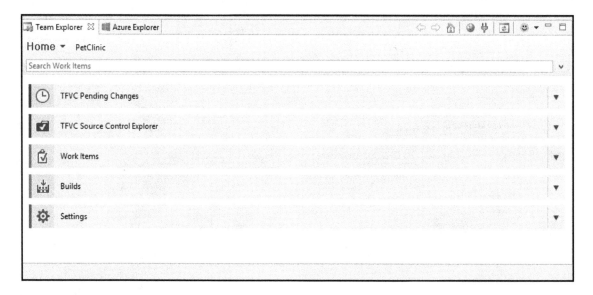

Click on **Add...** in the **Team Foundation Server** list. Provide the **URL** of our VSTS account:

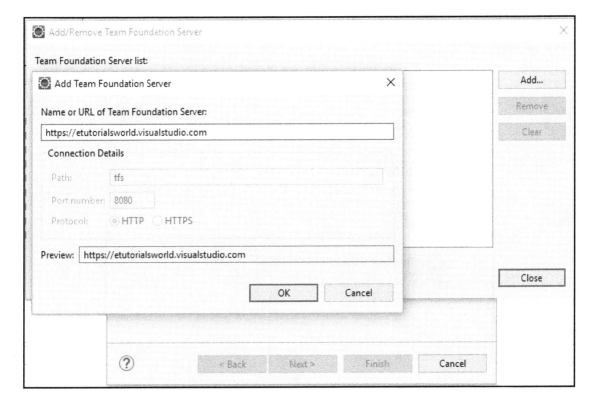

It will try to connect to the VSTS account and ask for credentials.

Once the connection is successful, we can connect to the server from Eclipse.

Click on **Next:**

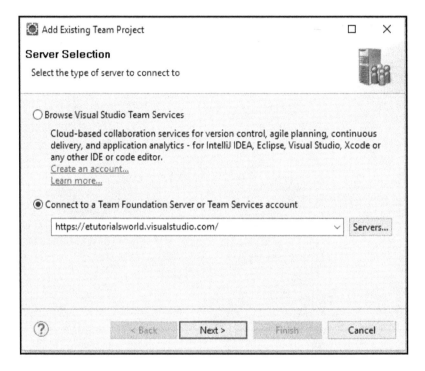

Select a **Team Project from the list.**

Click on **Finish**:

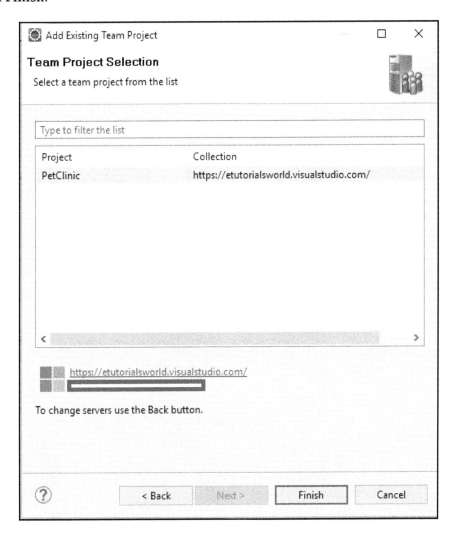

Go to the VSTS account in the browser and verify the existing data in the Project folder.

Verify the **Team Explorer** perspective in Eclipse. Now it is connected, so we can perform operations:

Before any other action, import a PetClinic code into Eclipse.

Right-click on the **Project** and click on **Team**.

Select Share Project.

Select **Team Foundation Server** in the **Select a repository type** plugin dialog box.

Click on **Next**:

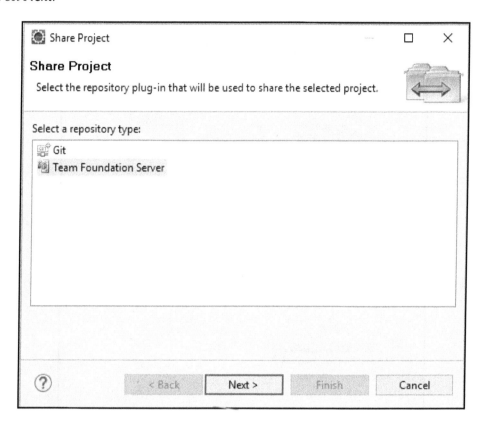

Select the team project that we created initially in the VSTS in the **Team Project Selection** dialog box:

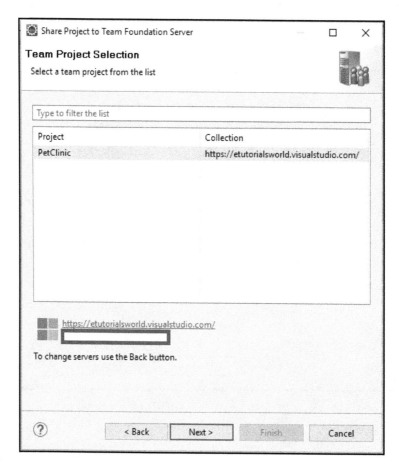

Select a server location to share the project:

Review the share configuration and click on **Finish**.

Once done, go to the **Team Explorer** perspective and click on **Check In** after providing a comment:

Confirm **Check In**.

Verify **Check In** in Eclipse, where the icons of the nearby files will be changed to denote that the files are not changed since the last check in process.

Verify all the files in VSTS:

Once we have the code available in the VSTS code section, we can easily configure continuous integration in VSTS.

Continuous integration in VSTS

Essentially, we will follow the process where developers can share code in the repository using IDE. VSTS will trigger a build definition execution and it will perform compilation of source files, unit test execution, and other tasks based on configuration and create a package file:

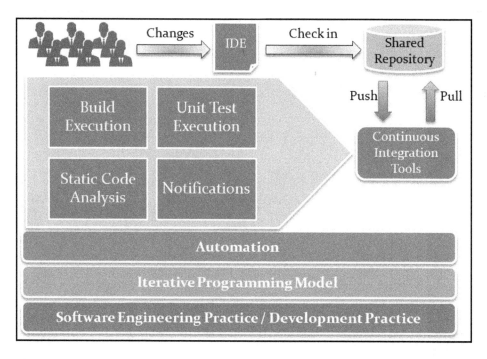

In VSTS, we need to create the build definition for continuous integration. Go to the VSTS account in the browser.

Click on the **PetClinic** project:

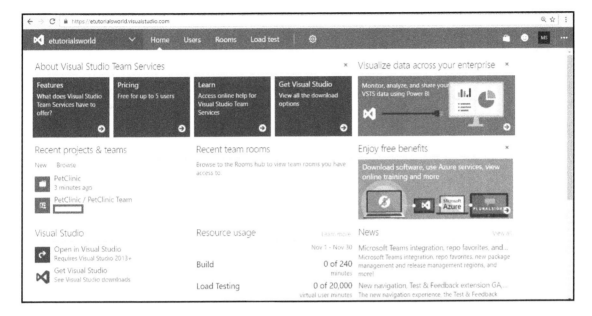

Click on the **Build & Release** menu in the top bar and select **Builds**:

There is no build definition available as of now. Create a **+ New Definition**:

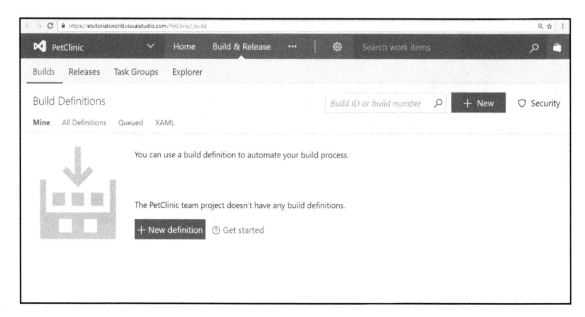

We have Maven-based projects, so we will select the **Maven** build definition template:

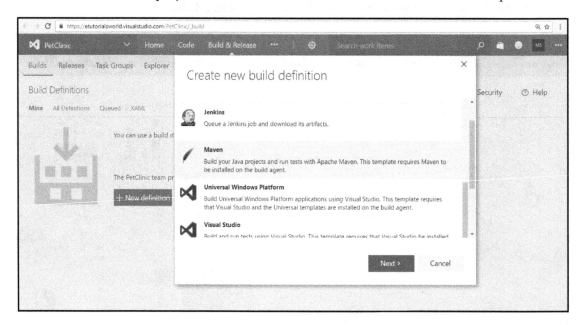

Select a **Repository source:**

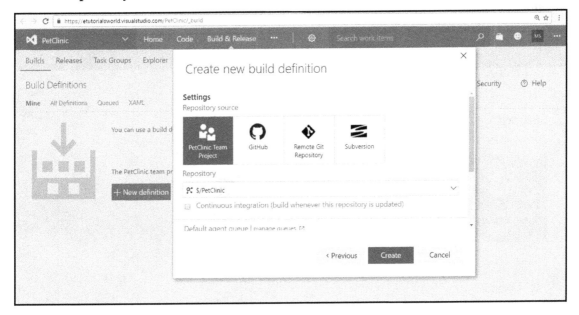

Check **Continuous Integration (build whenever this repository is updated)**. Click on **Create**:

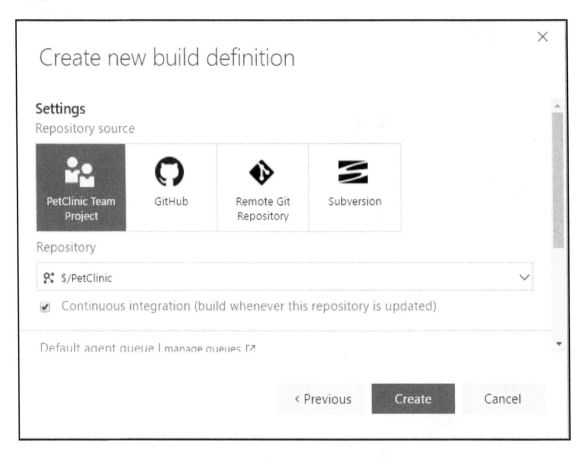

It will open the build definition in **Edit** mode.

In the Maven build step, verify the location of the pom.xml file:

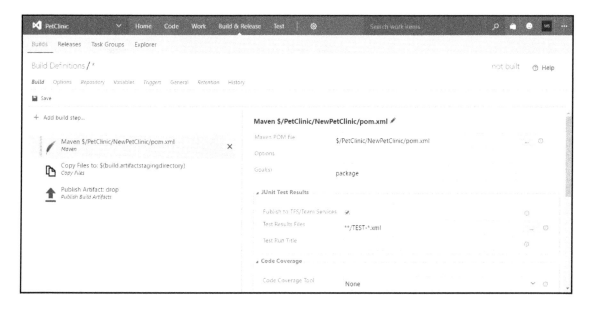

Click on the **Triggers** section and verify **Continuous integration (CI)**:

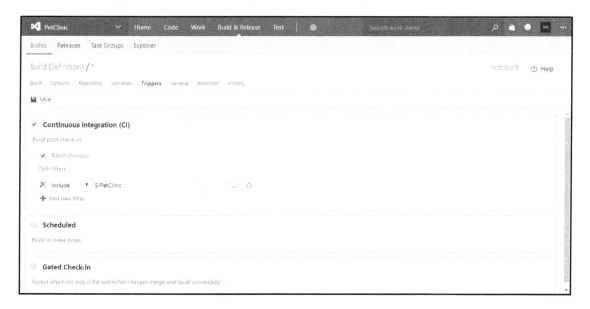

Click on the **Save** button and give an appropriate name to the build definition:

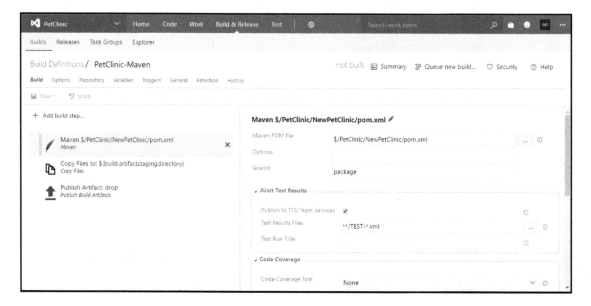

Click on **Queue new build...** to execute the build definition:

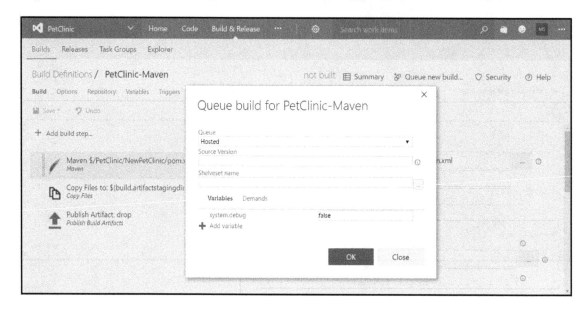

It will wait for the available agent to execute the build definition:

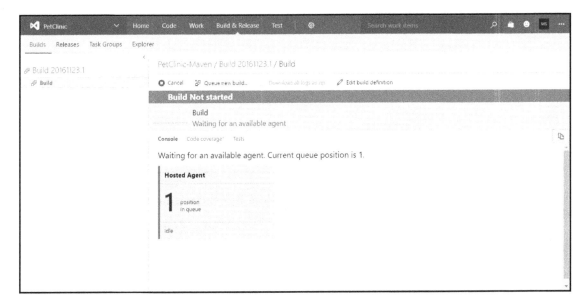

Wait until the build execution is completed successfully:

Go to the **Builds** section and verify the build results:

Verify the **Summary** of the build definition execution. It is executed on the hosted agent. All the required runtime is available on the hosted agent:

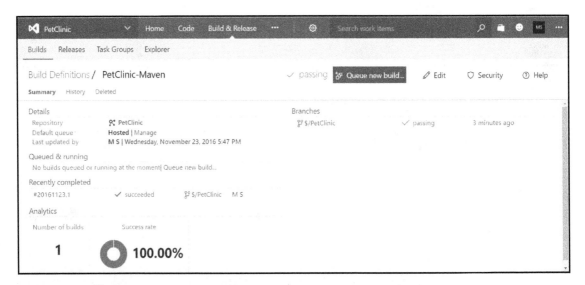

Verify the history of the build definition execution to find out the result of unit test execution:

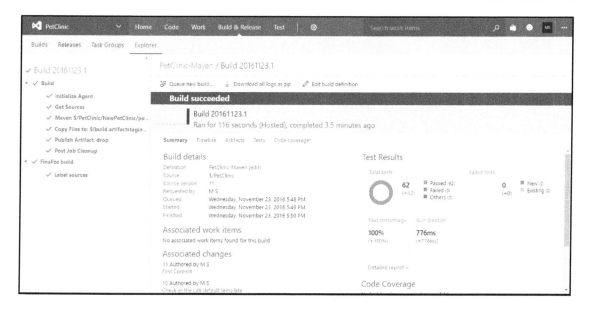

Go to the **Test Plans** section in VSTS and click on **Recent test runs** to find out more details on unit test execution:

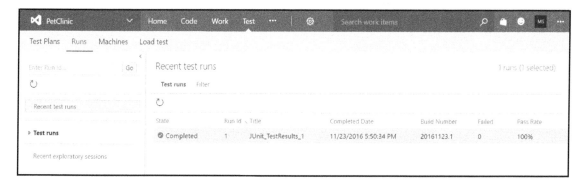

Now we are done.

We have used VSTS to achieve continuous integration for our sample spring-based Java web application.

Most of the things in Jenkins and VSTS are the same in terms of the way we perform automation. Hence, understanding of one tool always helps to do the same with any other tools and it proves our belief that it is not about tools. It is about people, processes, mindsets, and tools.

Summary

There is a famous quote by Marcel Proust that says:

> *The real voyage of discovery consists not in seeking new landscapes, but in having new eyes.*

We will change the way application packages are created. We may need to go through the same kind of procedures to create a package or a WAR file or an APK file or an IPA file. Hence, we are not seeking new landscape. However, we need to find an efficient way to finish the process effectively and hence we need to look for having new eyes.

In this chapter, we have described in detail how we can perform continuous integration using Jenkins and Visual Studio Team Services. We have seen results of the unit test execution and how packages are created in Jenkins and Visual Studio Team Services.

The most important thing we know is that we need to consider implementation of continuous integration as a DevOps practice doesn't require specific tools. We can use any tool for automation and achieve the same objective. It is about the culture or patterns in the organization and not the tools.

Once we have the package ready, we need to prepare or keep ready an environment for deployment. We will see how to prepare an environment using Docker containers in the next chapter.

3
Containers

"The first rule of any technology used in a business is that automation applied to an efficient operation will magnify the efficiency. The second is that automation applied to an inefficient operation will magnify the inefficiency."

- Bill Gates

We have seen DevOps practices and continuous integration until now. However, recently, containers have become a buzz word and everyone wants to have a hands-on experience with it. The main reason is to utilize the resources effectively and efficiently. Docker is an open source initiative for OS virtualization that automates the deployment of applications inside software containers. It is extremely useful to utilize containers for Dev or QA environments for better resource utilization.

In this chapter, we will try to install and create a sample container. The objective is to get familiar with Docker containers and get a feel of how containers can be utilized for application deployment.

This chapter provides a quick overview of containers. We will be focusing on the following topics in this chapter:

- Overview of Docker containers
- Understanding the difference between virtual machines and containers
- Installing and configuring Docker
- Creating a Tomcat container

Overview of Docker containers

Docker provides isolated user spaces and hence provides user-based processes, space, and filesystems. Behind the scenes, it shares the Linux host kernel. The following diagram illustrates the working mechanism of a Docker container:

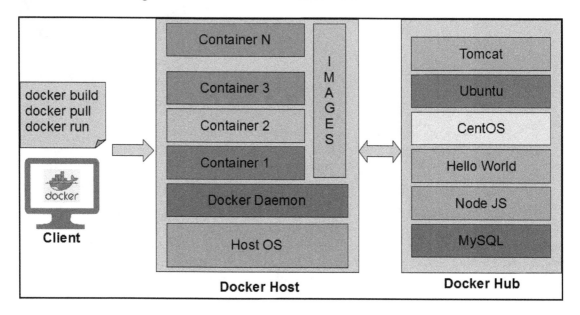

Docker has two main components with a client-server architecture:

- **Docker Host**
- **Docker Hub**

Let's take a look at them in more detail:

- **Docker Host**: The Docker Host contains the Docker daemon, containers, and images. The Docker engine is an important component that provides the core Docker technology. This core Docker technology enables images and containers. When we install Docker successfully, we run a simple command. In our case, we will consider CentOS for the container. To run an interactive shell in the CentOS image, use docker `run -i -t <image> /bin/bash`:
  - The `-i` flag initiates an interactive container
  - The `-t` flag creates a pseudoterminal that attaches `stdin` and `stdout`
  - The image is a CentOS image
  - `/bin/bash` starts a shell

  When we run this command, it verifies whether the CentOS image is available locally. If it is not available, it will download the image from Docker Hub.

  An image has a filesystem and parameter that can be used at runtime, while a container is an instance of an image with a state. It is simple to understand that containers change, while images do not.

- **Docker Hub**: Docker Hub is a **Software as a Service** (**SaaS**) for sharing and managing Docker containers. It is a kind of centralized registry service provided by Docker. As a user, we can use it to build and ship applications. It allows us to create a pipeline to integrate with code repositories and for collaboration, image discovery, and automation.

Understanding the difference between virtual machines and containers

Before we start installation of docker and creation of a container, it will be useful to get an understanding of why containers are different and how they are different from virtual machines.

Let's understand the basic difference between virtual machines and containers.

Virtual machines

In a **virtual machine (VM)**, we need to install an operating system with the appropriate device drivers; hence,the footprint or size of a virtual machine is huge. A normal VM with Tomcat and Java installed may take up to 10 GB of drive space:

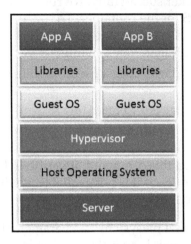

There's an overhead of memory management and device drivers. A VM has all the components a normal physical machine has in terms of operation.

In a VM, the hypervisor abstracts resources. Its package includes not only the application, but also the necessary binaries and libraries, and an entire guest operating system, for example, CentOS 6.7 and Windows 2003.

Cloud service providers use a hypervisor to provide a standard runtime environment for VMs. Hypervisors come in type 1 and type 2 categories.

Containers

A container shares the operating system and device drivers of the host. Containers are created from images, and for a container with Tomcat installed, the size is less than 500 MB:

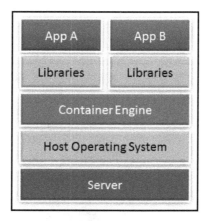

Containers are small in size and hence effectively give faster and better performance. They abstract the operating system.

A container runs as an isolated user space, with processes and filesystems in the user space on the host operating system itself, and it shares the kernel with other containers. Sharing and resource utilization are at their best in containers, and more resources are available due to less overhead. It works with very few required resources.

Docker makes it efficient and easier to port applications across environments.

Installing and configuring Docker

Let's quickly install the Docker on Windows 10. In our case, it is a Windows Home edition; so, we need to install Docker toolbox from `https://www.docker.com/products/docker-to olbox`:

1. Click on the **Download** button:

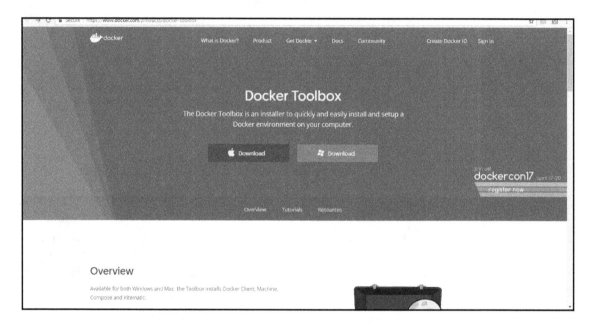

2. It will redirect you to `https://github.com/docker/toolbox/releases/tag/v1. 12.5` or the page with the latest version.

3. Download **DockerToolbox**. Click on the exe file of **Docker toolbox** to install it:

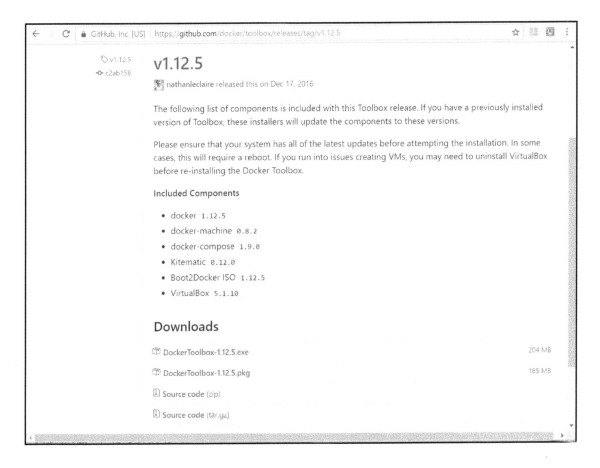

4. Click on Next > on the welcome page:

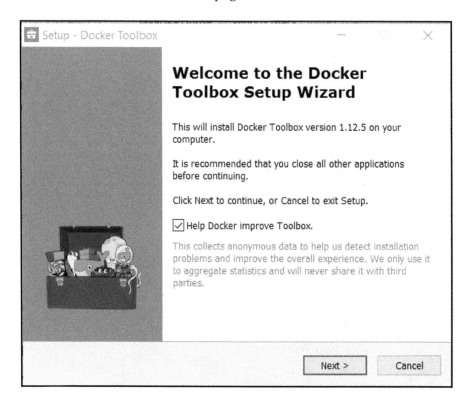

5. Select the preferred location to install **Docker Toolbox**:

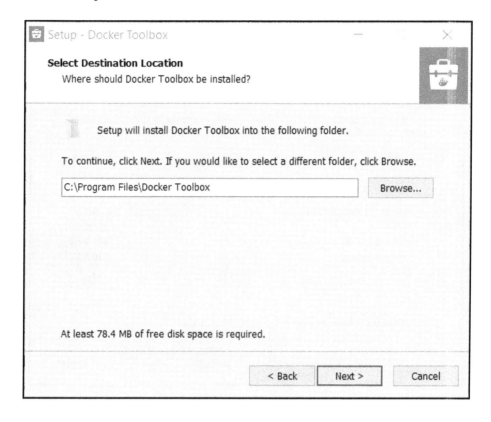

6. Keep all the default components for installation.

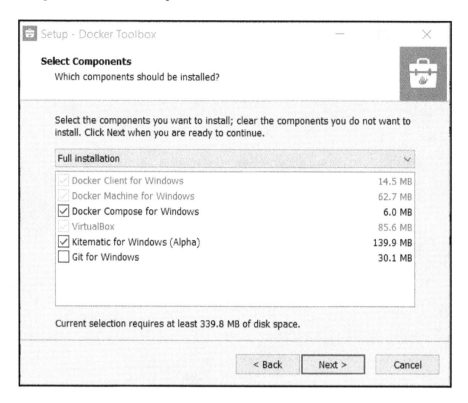

7. **Select Additional Tasks** that should be performed and click on **Next >**:

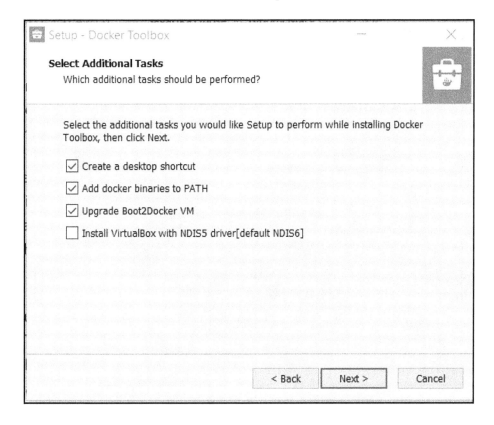

8. Click on **Install**:

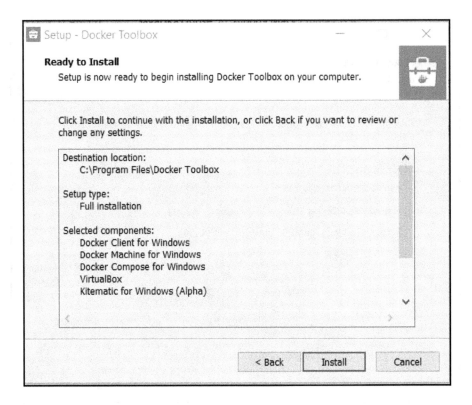

9. Docker toolbox installation will install the virtual box too:

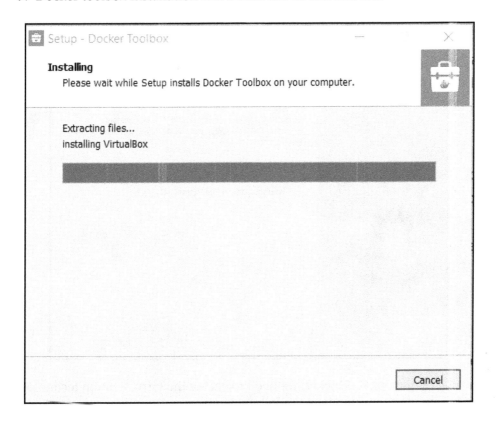

10. Click on **Finish**:

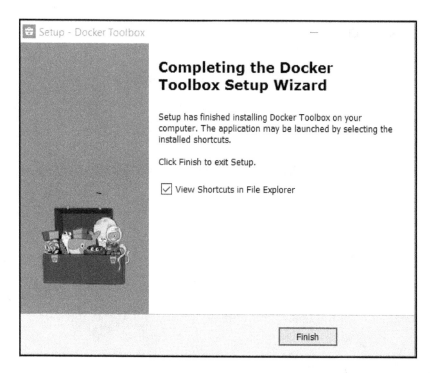

Before starting operations on Docker, we need to enable the virtualization technology in the Windows system, or else we will get the following error:

- Creating CA using `C:UsersMitesh.dockermachinecertsca.pem`
- Creating a client certificate
  using `C:UsersMitesh.dockermachinecertscert.pem`
- Running pre-create checks... Error with pre-create check: "This computer doesn't have VT-X/AMD-v enabled. Enabling it in the BIOS is mandatory" Looks like something went wrong in step 'Checking if machine default exists'... Press any key to continue...

- Go to **Settings** and click on **Advanced Startup**. **Restart the system. Change the BIOS setting to enable Virtualization Technology**:

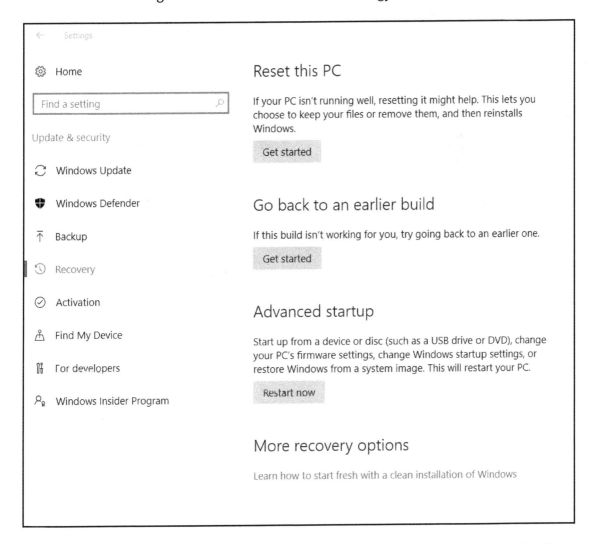

Once the system is restarted, click on **Docker Quickstart Terminal** on the desktop. It will run precreate checks and download `boot2docker.iso` and run the virtual machine.

After all proper configuration and checks, Docker is up and running:

```
Running pre-create checks...
Creating machine...
(default) Copying C:\Users\Mitesh\.docker\machine\cache\boot2docker.iso to C:\Users\Mitesh\.docker\machine\machines\default\boot2docker.iso...
(default) Creating VirtualBox VM...
(default) Creating SSH key...
(default) Starting the VM...
(default) Check network to re-create if needed...
(default) Windows might ask for the permission to create a network adapter. Sometimes, such confirmation window is minimized in the taskbar.
(default) Found a new host-only adapter: "VirtualBox Host-Only Ethernet Adapter #2"
(default) Windows might ask for the permission to configure a network adapter. Sometimes, such confirmation window is minimized in the taskbar.
(default) Windows might ask for the permission to configure a dhcp server. Sometimes, such confirmation window is minimized in the taskbar.
                                          (default) Waiting for an IP...
Waiting for machine to be running, this may take a few minutes...
Detecting operating system of created instance...
Waiting for SSH to be available...
Detecting the provisioner...
Provisioning with boot2docker...
Copying certs to the local machine directory...
Copying certs to the remote machine...
Setting Docker configuration on the remote daemon...
Checking connection to Docker...
Docker is up and running!
To see how to connect your Docker Client to the Docker Engine running on this virtual machine, run: C:\Program Files\Docker Toolbox\docker-machine.exe env def
ault


                 ##         .
           ## ## ##        ==
        ## ## ## ## ##    ===
    /"""""""""""""""""\___/ ===
~~~ {~~ ~~~~ ~~~ ~~~~ ~~~ ~ /  ===- ~~~
    _____ o           __/
     \    \         __/
      _____/


     is configured to use the default machine with IP 192.168.99.100
For help getting started, check out the docs at https://docs.docker.com

Start interactive shell
```

 To get details on how to install Docker in CentOS, read *DevOps for web development*, available at `https://www.packtpub.com/networking-and-servers/devops-web-development`.

Once **Docker is up and running,** we are ready to create docker containers. Note the IP address of the default docker machine:

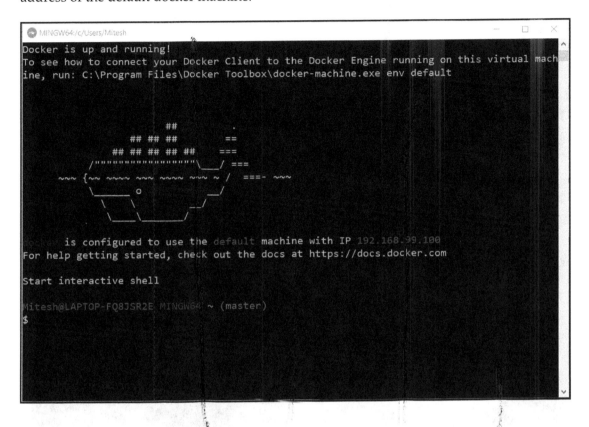

Let's create a sample hello world container. Execute `docker run hello-world`. If you get the `"Hello from Docker!"` message, then we have created the container successfully:

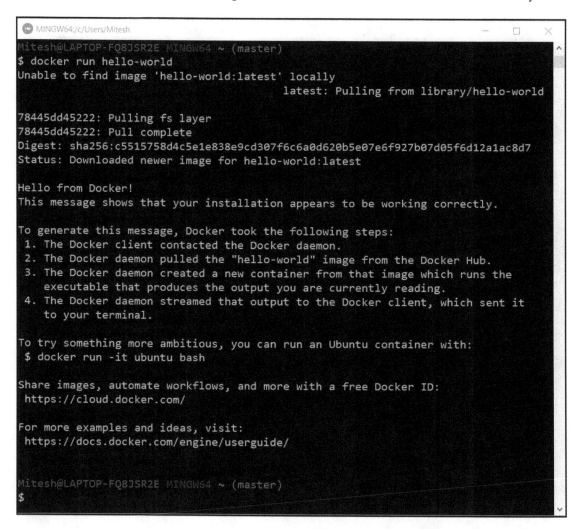

As we need to deploy a JEE application, we will create a Tomcat container in the next section.

Creating a Tomcat container

In this section, we will create a container with the Tomcat web server installed so that we can deploy Java-based web applications into it:

1. Create an account in Docker hub and **Login**:

2. We can search different images from the Docker hub:

3. You can find the Tomcat image at `https://hub.docker.com/_/tomcat/`.

4. Use Docker's `pull` command to get the Tomcat image:

   ```
   docker pull tomcat
   ```

5. Once the Tomcat image is available, verify it using the `docker images` command:

6. To run docker container from the image, run `docker run -it --rm -p 8888:8080 tomcat:8.0`.

7. Use the IP address of the default docker machine and port 8888 in the browser to verify whether Tomcat is running properly in the container or not:

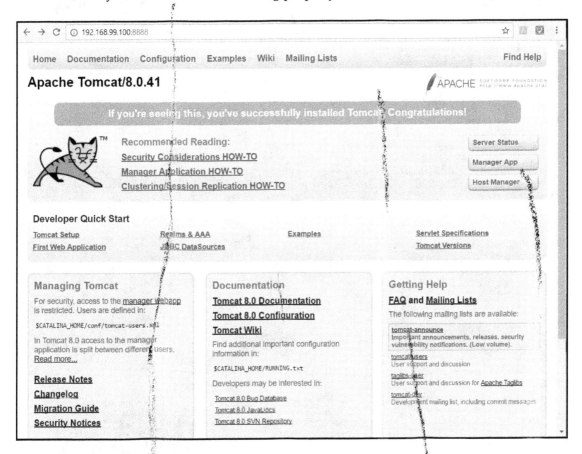

8. To get the IP address of the virtual machine, execute `docker-machine ls` command.

Let's verify whether we have access to the Tomcat manager application in this container:

```
Mitesh@LAPTOP-FQ8JSR2E MINGW64 ~ (master)
$ docker-machine ls
NAME      ACTIVE    DRIVER       STATE      URL                          SWARM    DOCKER       ERRORS
default   *         virtualbox   Running    tcp://192.168.99.100:2376             v17.03.0-ce

Mitesh@LAPTOP-FQ8JSR2E MINGW64 ~ (master)
$ docker run --rm tomcat cat conf/tomcat-users.xml
<?xml version='1.0' encoding='utf-8'?>
<!--
  Licensed to the Apache Software Foundation (ASF) under one or more
  contributor license agreements.  See the NOTICE file distributed with
  this work for additional information regarding copyright ownership.
  The ASF licenses this file to You under the Apache License, Version 2.0
  (the "License"); you may not use this file except in compliance with
  the License.  You may obtain a copy of the License at

      http://www.apache.org/licenses/LICENSE-2.0

  Unless required by applicable law or agreed to in writing, software
  distributed under the License is distributed on an "AS IS" BASIS,
  WITHOUT WARRANTIES OR CONDITIONS OF ANY KIND, either express or implied.
  See the License for the specific language governing permissions and
  limitations under the License.
-->
<tomcat-users xmlns="http://tomcat.apache.org/xml"
              xmlns:xsi="http://www.w3.org/2001/XMLSchema-instance"
              xsi:schemaLocation="http://tomcat.apache.org/xml tomcat-users.xsd"
              version="1.0">
<!--
  NOTE:  By default, no user is included in the "manager-gui" role required
  to operate the "/manager/html" web application.  If you wish to use this app,
  you must define such a user - the username and password are arbitrary. It is
  strongly recommended that you do NOT use one of the users in the commented out
  section below since they are intended for use with the examples web
  application.
-->
<!--
  NOTE:  The sample user and role entries below are intended for use with the
  examples web application. They are wrapped in a comment and thus are ignored
  when reading this file. If you wish to configure these users for use with the
  examples web application, do not forget to remove the <!.. ..> that surrounds
  them. You will also need to set the passwords to something appropriate.
-->
<!--
  <role rolename="tomcat"/>
  <role rolename="role1"/>
  <user username="tomcat" password="<must-be-changed>" roles="tomcat"/>
  <user username="both" password="<must-be-changed>" roles="tomcat,role1"/>
  <user username="role1" password="<must-be-changed>" roles="role1"/>
-->
```

What we will do here is, create a new image with our own `tomcat-users.xml`, where we will create a user with the `manager-script` role to access the Tomcat manager application.

Create a directory. Go to that directory and create a `tomcat-users.xml` file.

Add the following content in it:

```
<?xml version='1.0' encoding='utf-8'?>
<tomcat-users
xmlns="http://tomcat.apache.org/xml" xmlns:xsi="http://www.w3.org/2001/XMLS
chema-instance"
xsi:schemaLocation="http://tomcat.apache.org/xml tomcat-
users.xsd" version="1.0">
<!--
NOTE: The sample user and role entries below are intended for use
with the examples web application. They are wrapped in a comment and thus
are ignored when reading this file. If you wish to configure these users
for use with the examples web application, do not forget to remove the
<!....> that surrounds them. You will also need to set the passwords to
something appropriate.
-->
<role rolename="manager-script"/>
<user username="admin" password="admin@123" roles="manager-script"/>
</tomcat-users>
```

Create a new file with the name `Dockerfile` in the same directory and add the following content:

```
FROM tomcat:8.0
MAINTAINER Mitesh<xxxxxx.xxxxxx@gmail.com>
COPY tomcat-users.xml /usr/local/tomoat/conf/tomcat-users.xml
```

In the **Docker Quickstart Terminal**, go to the directory that we have created.

Execute `docker build -t devops_tomcat_sc .`

Once the image is successfully built, verify it using docker images:

```
MINGW64:/c/Users/Mitesh/Desktop/Tomcat                                    —    □    ×
Mitesh@LAPTOP-FQ8JSR2E MINGW64 ~/Desktop/Tomcat (master)
$ docker build -t devops_tomcat_sc .
Sending build context to Docker daemon 3.584 kB
Step 1/3 : FROM tomcat:8.0
 ---> 4452dae04daa
Step 2/3 : MAINTAINER Mitesh<mitesh.soni83@gmail.com>
 ---> Running in f8bd1ee150b0
 ---> 3673892f552b
Removing intermediate container f8bd1ee150b0
Step 3/3 : COPY tomcat-users.xml /usr/local/tomcat/conf/tomcat-users.xml
 ---> b08d3e1add28
Removing intermediate container 972bbb81312e
Successfully built b08d3e1add28
SECURITY WARNING: You are building a Docker image from Windows against a non-Windows Docker host. All files and director
ies added to build context will have '-rwxr-xr-x' permissions. It is recommended to double check and reset permissions f
or sensitive files and directories.

Mitesh@LAPTOP-FQ8JSR2E MINGW64 ~/Desktop/Tomcat (master)
$ docker images
REPOSITORY          TAG           IMAGE ID          CREATED           SIZE
devops_tomcat_sc    latest        b08d3e1add28      15 seconds ago    355.4 MB
tomcat              8.0           4452dae04daa      12 days ago       355.4 MB
tomcat              latest        4452dae04daa      12 days ago       355.4 MB
hello-world         latest        48b5124b2768      8 weeks ago       1.84 kB
```

Execute `docker run -it -p 8888:8080 devops_tomcat_sc:8.0` and verify the number of containers using `docker ps -a`.

We can stop the container using `docker stop <container_name>`:

```
Mitesh@LAPTOP-FQ8JSR2E MINGW64 ~ (master)
$ docker ps -a
CONTAINER ID    IMAGE               COMMAND             CREATED           STATUS                    PORTS                      NAMES
9d3d297ffe47    devops_tomcat_sc    "catalina.sh run"   51 minutes ago    Up 51 minutes             0.0.0.0:9999->8080/tcp     zealous_mcnulty
302903126e3c    hello-world         "/hello"            2 hours ago       Exited (0) 2 hours ago                               gracious_dubinsky

Mitesh@LAPTOP-FQ8JSR2E MINGW64 ~ (master)
$ docker stop zealous_mcnulty
zealous_mcnulty

Mitesh@LAPTOP-FQ8JSR2E MINGW64 ~ (master)
$ docker ps -a
CONTAINER ID    IMAGE               COMMAND             CREATED           STATUS                      PORTS            NAMES
9d3d297ffe47    devops_tomcat_sc    "catalina.sh run"   52 minutes ago    Exited (143) 5 seconds ago                   zealous_mcnulty
302903126e3c    hello-world         "/hello"            2 hours ago       Exited (0) 2 hours ago                       gracious_dubinsky

Mitesh@LAPTOP-FQ8JSR2E MINGW64 ~ (master)
$
```

To change the name of the container, use `docker run -it -p 9999:8080 --name bootcamp_tomcat devops_tomcat_sc`.

Verify the name using `docker ps -a`:

Use the virtual machine IP address and `9999` as a port number to access Tomcat running in the container:

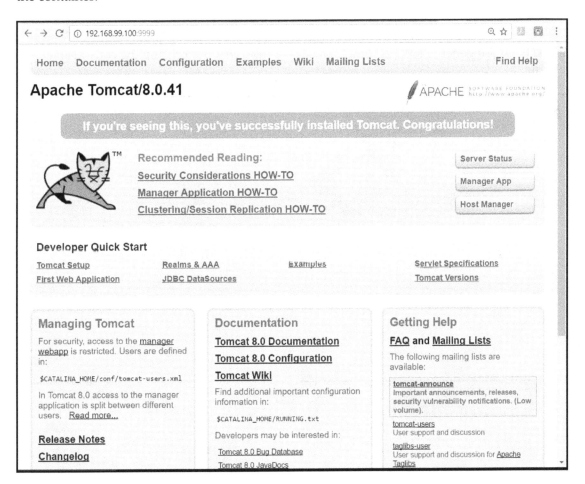

Verify the manager access with the `manager-script` role using the following URL:

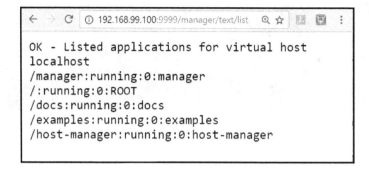

Let's just try to deploy an application using the `Deploy to Container` plugin in Tomcat. If one build job generates WAR files, then copy it from that build using the copy artifact plugin:

In **Post-build Actions**, select **Deploy war/ear to a container**. Give the username and password provided in **tomcat-users.xml**. Give the Tomcat URL. Click on **Apply/Save**:

Click on **Build Now**:

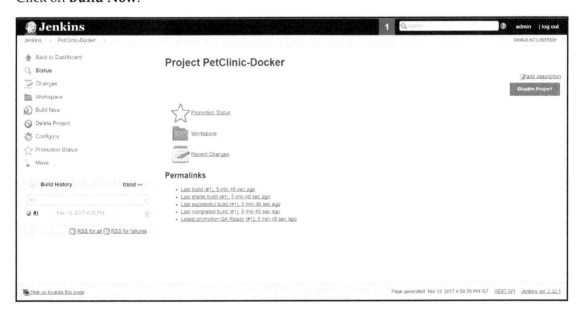

Go to **Console Output** and verify the deployment process:

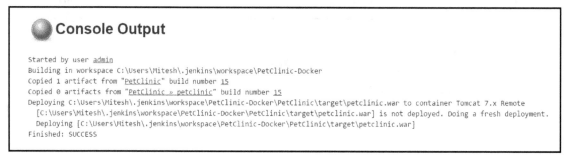

Verify the application URL using the Tomcat URL and application context:

Now we are done.

Thus you can see that we have created an image, a container, and deployed the application in the Tomcat container.

Summary

So we have seen in this chapter how to install Docker containers in Windows 10, and how to use Docker hub to find images available in the public domain.

We have executed the hello world container to verify whether Docker has been successfully installed or not. Once we have verified the Docker installation, we used Docker hub to get the Tomcat image and successfully created a Tomcat 8 container and accessed it through the browser.

We also used Jenkins to deploy the application in the Tomcat container. Our objective was to utilize the docker container for application deployment.

In the next chapter, we will cover how we can utilize the configuration management tool Chef for setting up the run-time environment so that we can deploy Java-based web applications in the virtual machine.

4

Cloud Computing and Configuration Management

"Change is hard because people overestimate the value of what they have and underestimate the value of what they may gain by giving that up."

— *James Belasco and Ralph Stayer*

In the previous chapter, we have seen an overview of Docker containers. In this chapter, we will focus on creating and configuring the environment for application deployment in the cloud. We will use **Infrastructure as a Service** (**IaaS**) and the configuration management tool, Chef, to create a platform so that we can deploy an application in the later part using automation.

Chef is a configuration management tool that can be utilized to create a runtime environment for application deployment on a physical machine, virtualized infrastructure, or in the public or private cloud infrastructure.

In this chapter, we will cover the following topics:

- An overview of the Chef configuration management tool
- Installing and configuring a Chef workstation
- Converging a Chef node using a Chef workstation
- Installing Tomcat packages using community cookbooks

An overview of the Chef configuration management tool

Chef is one of the most popular configuration tools. It comes in two flavors:

- Open source Chef server
- Hosted Chef

What we intend to do here is to show how to prepare a runtime environment for application deployment. Let's understand it in terms of application life cycle management:

1. We have a Java-based Spring application package ready after continuous integration.
2. We need to deploy the application in the Tomcat web server.
3. The Tomcat server can be installed in a physical system, virtualized environment, Amazon EC2 instances, or Microsoft Azure virtual machines.
4. We also need to install Java.

In all these, except for the first point, we need to do the installation and configuration activity manual avoid such a repetitive scenario, we can use the Chef configuration management tool to create a virtual machine in AWS or in Microsoft Azure and then install Tomcat with all the dependencies in order to deploy our Java-based spring application.

However, let's look at the basics of the Chef configuration management tool so that we can understand how Chef works and how it performs various steps.

There are three important parts of the Chef configuration management tool:

- **The open source Chef server or hosted Chef**: The Chef server installed on-premise or the hosted Chef, is the heart of this automation process of installing the runtime environment. It is a centralized repository of cookbooks and details of registered nodes. A Chef workstation is used to upload cookbooks and make changes in the configurations so that they can be applied to the nodes available in the AWS and Microsoft Azure.
- **The Chef workstation**: A Chef workstation is a system where we can manage cookbooks and other changes. We can perform all the administrative tasks from the Chef workstation. Knife is used to upload cookbooks to the Chef server and execute plugin commands. Knife plugins can be used to perform various operations in AWS and Microsoft Azure Cloud.

- **Node**: A node is a physical or virtual machine. This virtual machine can be in a virtualized environment, a private cloud empowered by Openstack or VMware, or in a public cloud such as AWS or Microsoft Azure:
  - The node communicates with the open source or hosted Chef server
  - Node gets the configuration details related to itself, and then starts executing the steps based on these to maintain itself in compliance with what the administrator has decided

Go to the official Chef website at `https://chef.io` and visit the Chef homepage. We can use the on-premise Chef server by installing and managing it on our own or we can use the hosted Chef:

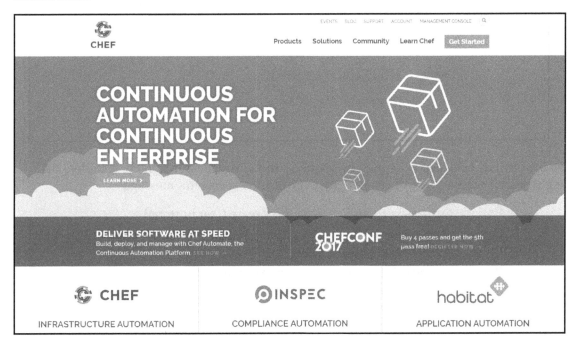

1. Click on **MANAGEMENT CONSOLE** on `https://chef.io` or navigate to `https://manage.chef.io/login`.
2. On `https://manage.chef.io/login` click on **Click here to get started!**.
3. Provide the **Full Name**, **Company** name, **Email ID**, and **Username.**
4. Check the box that says **I agree to the Terms of Service and the Master License and Services Agreement.**
5. Click on the **Get Started** button.

Refer to the following screenshot:

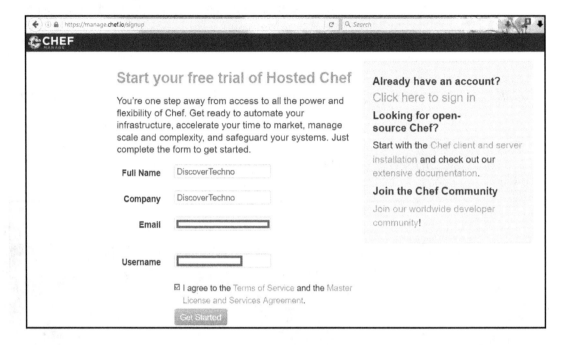

So the obvious next step is to go to the mailbox and verify the e-mail ID to complete the registration process. We will get an e-mail verification successful message:

1. Provide the password and click on the **Create User** button.
2. Now create an organization.
3. Click on **Create New Organization.**
4. Provide the **Full Name** and **Short Name** of the organization.
5. Click on the **Create Organization** button.

Refer to the following screenshot:

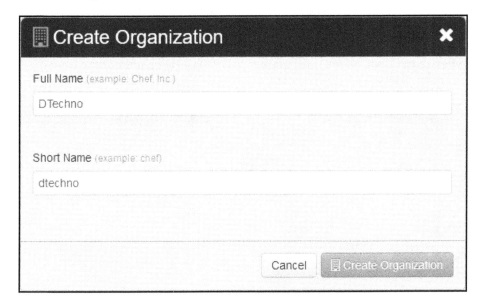

Now, download a starter kit:

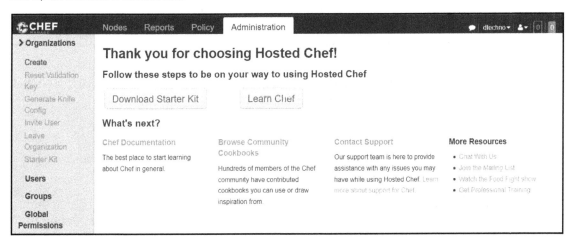

1. Click on **Download Starter Kit**.
2. We will get confirmation dialog; click on **Proceed**.
3. Let's verify the operations available on the hosted Chef.

4. We haven't configured any node, so the node list is empty. Click on **Nodes**. Once we create the node and register it, we will get all the details about that node in the Chef server or on the hosted Chef.

5. Go to the **Administration** menu and click on **Users** in the sidebar.

6. Verify the **User Name**, **Full Name**, and **Email** ID created at the time of registration:

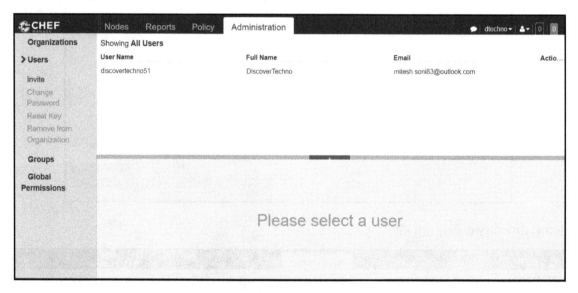

Check the **Reports** tab and we won't find any data. The reason for this is that the process of convergence, where nodes become compliant based on the configuration available on the Chef server, has not taken place and hence there is no data.

At this stage, we have a hosted Chef account available.

Now, let's configure a Chef workstation so that we can communicate with the hosted Chef and converge the nodes in AWS and Microsoft Azure Cloud:

1. Based on the operating system, download the Chef client installable file. In our case, we are using CentOS; therefore, we will download the Red Hat version of the Chef client from `https://downloads.chef.io/chef-client/redhat/`.

2. Select the operating system type.

3. Select the Chef client version.

4. Download the installation files.

The Chef-dk or Chef development kit is used for installing development tools, and it can also be used to install knife plugins for AWS and Microsoft Azure. Download it from `https://downloads.chef.io/chef-dk/`. This will help us to install `knife-ec2` and `knife-azure` plugins so that we can create and manage virtual machines in the cloud environment.

Once we have installable files ready for the Chef client and Chef development kit and the hosted Chef account is also available, it is time to install and configure the Chef workstation. Let's do it in the next section.

Installing and configuring a Chef workstation

Let's verify whether the Chef client has been installed on the system or virtual machine where we want to configure the Chef workstation:

1. Execute the `chef-client -version` command; if we get the command not found error, then it means that the Chef client is not installed. If the Chef client is installed, then it will give the version number:

   ```
   [mitesh@devops1 Desktop]$ chef-client -version
   bash: chef-client: command not found
   ```

2. Go to the directory where the Chef client installable is downloaded:

   ```
   [mitesh@devops1 Desktop]$ cd chef/
   [mitesh@devops1 chef]$ ls
   chef-12.9.41-1.el6.x86_64.rpmchefdk-0.13.21-
   1.el6.x86_64.rpm
   ```

3. Run the Chef client RPM using `rpm -ivh chef-<version>.rpm`:

   ```
   [mitesh@devops1 chef]$ rpm -ivh chef-12.9.41-
   1.el6.x86_64.rpm
   warning: chef-12.9.41-1.el6.x86_64.rpm: Header
   V4DSA/SHA1 Signature, key ID
   83ef826a: NOKEY
   error: can't create transaction lock on
   /var/lib/rpm/.rpm.lock (Permission
   denied)
   ```

4. If the permission is denied while installing the Chef RPM, then use `sudo` to run the command:

```
[mitesh@devops1 chef]$ sudo rpm -ivh chef-12.9.41-
1.el6.x86_64.rpm
[sudo] password for mitesh:
warning: chef-12.9.41-1.el6.x86_64.rpm: Header
V4DSA/SHA1 Signature, key ID
83ef826a: NOKEY
Preparing...
######################################### [100%]
1:chef
######################################### [100%]
Thank you for installing Chef!
```

5. After successful installation, verify the Chef client version and this time we will get the version number of the Chef client:

```
[mitesh@devops1 chef]$ chef-client -version
Chef: 12.9.41
```

Now we will use the Chef starter kit that we downloaded while creating an account in the hosted Chef:

1. Extract `chef-repo`. Copy the `.chef` directory into the root or user folder:

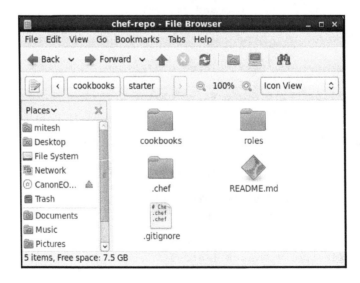

2. Verify the `cookbooks` folder available in the `chef-repo` directory:

3. In the `.chef` folder, open the `knife.rb` file in the editor, which contains various configurations. Modify the path of the cookbooks directory if required:

```
current_dir = File.dirname(__FILE__)
log_level                   :info
log_locationSTDOUT
node_name"discovertechno51"
client_key"#{current_dir}/discovertechno51.pem"
validation_client_name"dtechno-validator"
validation_key"#{current_dir}/dtechno-validator.pem"
chef_server_url"https://api.chef.io/organizations/dtechno"
cookbook_path               ["#{current_dir}/../cookbooks"]
```

With that, we've finished configuring our Chef workstation. The next step is using it to converge the node.

Converging a Chef node using a Chef workstation

In this section, we will set up the runtime environment in the node (physical/virtual machine) using the Chef workstation.

Log in to the Chef workstation:

1. Open the terminal and verify the IP address by executing the `ifconfig` command:

    ```
    [root@devops1 chef-repo]#ifconfig
    eth3        Link encap:EthernetHWaddr00:0C:29:D9:30:7F
    inetaddr:192.168.1.35Bcast:192.168.1.255Mask:255.255.255.0
    inet6addr: fe80::20c:29ff:fed9:307f/64 Scope:Link
               UP BROADCAST RUNNING MULTICAST  MTU:1500Metric:1
               RX packets:841351errors:0dropped:0overruns:0frame:0
               TX packets:610551errors:0dropped:0overruns:0carrier:0
    collisions:0txqueuelen:1000
               RX bytes:520196141 (496.0 MiB)
               TX bytes:278125183 (265.2 MiB)
    lo         Link encap:Local Loopback
    inetaddr:127.0.0.1Mask:255.0.0.0
    inet6addr: ::1/128 Scope:Host
               UP LOOPBACK RUNNING  MTU:65536Metric:1
               RX packets:1680errors:0dropped:0overruns:0frame:0
               TX packets:1680errors:0dropped:0overruns:0carrier:0
    collisions:0txqueuelen:0
               RX bytes:521152 (508.9 KiB)  TX bytes:521152 (508.9 KiB)
    ```

2. Verify the knife version installed on the Chef workstation with `knife --version`:

    ```
    [root@devops1 chef]#knife --version
    Chef: 12.9.41
    ```

3. The `knife node list` command is used to obtain the list of nodes served by the Chef server in our case, the hosted Chef. As we haven't converged any nodes, the list will be empty:

    ```
    [root@devops1 chef-repo]#knife node list
    ```

4. Create a virtual machine using VMware Workstation or VirtualBox. Install CentOS. Once the VM is ready, find its IP address and note it down.

5. On our Chef workstation, open a terminal and, using the `ssh` command, try to connect to the node or VM we just created:

    ```
    [root@devops1 chef-repo]#sshroot@192.168.1.37
    The authenticity of the host 192.168.1.37 can't be established:
    RSA key fingerprint is
    4b:56:28:62:53:59:e8:e0:5e:5f:54:08:c1:0c:1e:6c.
    ```

```
Are you sure you want to continue connecting (yes/no)? yes
Warning: Permanently added '192.168.1.37' (RSA)
to the list of known hosts.
root@192.168.1.37's password:
Last login: Thu May 28 10:26:06 2015 from 192.168.1.15
```

6. We now have an SSH session on the node from the Chef workstation. If you
   verify the IP address, you'll know that you are accessing a different machine by
   remote (SSH) access:

```
[root@localhost ~]#ifconfig
eth1       Link encap:EthernetHWaddr00:0C:29:44:9B:4B
inetaddr:192.168.1.37Bcast:192.168.1.255Mask:255.255.255.0
inet6addr: fe80::20c:29ff:fe44:9b4b/64 Scope:Link
           UP BROADCAST RUNNING MULTICAST  MTU:1500Metric:1
           RX packets:11252errors:0dropped:0overruns:0frame:0
           TX packets:6628errors:0dropped:0overruns:0carrier:0
collisions:0txqueuelen:1000
           RX bytes:14158681 (13.5 MiB)   TX bytes:466365 (455.4 KiB)
lo         Link encap:Local Loopback
inetaddr:127.0.0.1Mask:255.0.0.0
inet6addr:  ::1/128 Scope:Host
           UP LOOPBACK RUNNING  MTU:65536Metric:1
           RX packets:59513errors:0dropped:0overruns:0frame:0
           TX packets:59513errors:0dropped:0overruns:0carrier:0
collisions:0txqueuelen:0
           RX bytes:224567119 (214.1 MiB)
           TX bytes:224567119 (214.1 MiB)
[root@localhost ~]#
```

7. Use knife to converge the node. Provide the IP address/DNS name, user,
   password, and name of the node.

8. Verify the output:

```
[root@devops1 chef-repo]# knife bootstrap
192.168.1.37 -x root -P cloud@123 -
N tomcatserver
Doing old-style registration with the validation
key at /home/mitesh/chef-
repo/.chef/dtechno-validator.pem...
Delete your validation key in order to use your
user credentials instead
Connecting to 192.168.1.37
192.168.1.37 -----> Installing Chef Omnibus (-v 12)
192.168.1.37 downloading
https://omnitruck-direct.chef.io/chef/install.sh
```

```
192.168.1.37   to file /tmp/install.sh.26574/install.sh
192.168.1.37 trying wget...
192.168.1.37 el 6 x86_64
192.168.1.37 Getting information for chef stable 12 for el...
192.168.1.37 downloading https://omnitruck-
direct.chef.io/stable/chef/metadata?v=12&p=el&pv=6&m=x86_64
192.168.1.37   to file /tmp/install.sh.26586/metadata.txt
192.168.1.37 trying wget...
192.168.1.37 sha1859bc9be9a40b8b13fb88744079ceef1832831b0
192.168.1.37
sha256c43f48e5a2de56e4eda473a3e
e0a80aa1aaa6c8621d9084e033d8b9cf3efc328
192.168.1.37 urlhttps://packages.chef.io/stable/el/6/chef-12.9.41-
1.el6.x86_64.rpm
192.168.1.37 version12.9.41
192.168.1.37 downloaded metadata file looks valid...
192.168.1.37 downloading
https://packages.chef.io/stable/el/6/chef-12.9.41-
1.el6.x86_64.rpm
192.168.1.37   to file /tmp/install.sh.26586/chef-
12.9.41-1.el6.x86_64.rpm
192.168.1.37 trying wget...
192.168.1.37 Comparing checksum with sha256sum...
192.168.1.37 Installing chef 12
192.168.1.37 installing with rpm...
192.168.1.37 warning: /tmp/install.sh.26586/chef-
12.9.41-1.el6.x86_64.rpm:
Header V4DSA/SHA1 Signature, key ID 83ef826a: NOKEY
192.168.1.37 Preparing...
        ######################################### [100%]
192.168.1.37    1:chef
        ######################################### [100%]
192.168.1.37 Thank you for installing Chef!
192.168.1.37 Starting the first Chef Client run...
192.168.1.37 Starting Chef Client, version 12.9.41
192.168.1.37 Creating a new client identity for
tomcatserver using the validator key.
192.168.1.37 resolving cookbooks for run list: []
192.168.1.37 Synchronizing Cookbooks:
192.168.1.37 Installing Cookbook Gems:
192.168.1.37 Compiling Cookbooks...
192.168.1.37 [2016-05-12T23:47:49-07:00] WARN:
Node tomcatserver has an empty
run list.
192.168.1.37 Converging 0 resources
192.168.1.37
192.168.1.37 Running handlers:
192.168.1.37 Running handlers complete
```

```
192.168.1.37 Chef Client finished, 0/0 resources
updated in 37 seconds
```

9. The node convergence is successful:
    1. Verify the first Chef client run in the log.
    2. Verify the Chef client version that is installed.
    3. Verify the empty run list message in the log.
    4. Verify converging 0 resource messages.

10. We can check whether the preceding process is successful or not by navigating to the hosted Chef account and verifying whether **Node Name** and **IP Address** in the **Nodes** section is available or not.

11. In the dashboard, go to the **Details** tab to get more information about the node; verify **Attributes** associated with the node and also **Permissions**:

12. In the bottom section of the hosted Chef **Dashboard**, verify the CPU attributes and other details of the node.

13. The report section provides details on **Runs Summary**, **Run Durations**, and **Run Counts**:

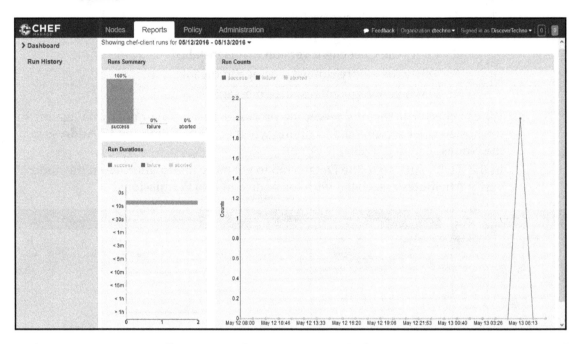

In the next section, we will try to install Tomcat using Chef.

Installing software packages using cookbooks

Until now, we've performed the following tasks:

- Creating a hosted Chef account
- Configuring a Chef workstation
- Converging a node using a Chef workstation

Now we will install application packages using community cookbooks.

To set up the runtime environment automatically, it's best to use the Chef community cookbooks:

1. Visit `https://github.com/chef-cookbooks` and find all the community cookbooks required to set up a runtime environment.

2. We are using a sample Spring application, namely, PetClinic. We need to install Java and Tomcat to run Java EE applications such as this.

3. Download the Tomcat cookbook from `https://supermarket.chef.io/cookbooks/tomcat` and navigate to the **Dependencies** section on that page. Without the dependencies uploaded to our Chef server, we can't upload the Tomcat cookbook to use it.

4. Download OpenSSL and Chef sugar from `https://supermarket.chef.io/cookbooks/openssl` and `https://supermarket.chef.io/cookbooks/chef-sugar` respectively.

5. To install Java, download the cookbook from `https://supermarket.chef.io/cookbooks/java` and its dependency as well from `https://supermarket.chef.io/cookbooks/apt`. Extract all the compressed files to the cookbook's directory:

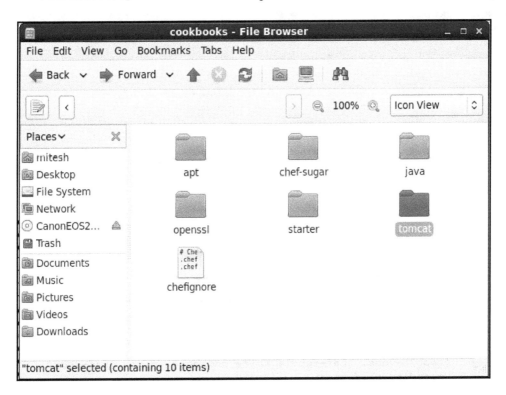

6. Go to cookbooks in the terminal and execute the `ls` command to verify the subdirectories of the community cookbooks which we downloaded earlier:

```
[root@devops1 cookbooks]# ls
apt  chefignore  chef-sugar  java  openssl  starter  tomcat
[root@devops1 cookbooks]# cd ..
```

7. Let's upload one of the cookbooks and verify whether it is uploaded on the hosted Chef or not. Upload the apt cookbook with the `knife cookbook upload apt` command as shown here:

```
[root@devops1 chef-repo]# knife cookbook upload apt
Uploading apt          [3.0.0]
Uploaded 1 cookbook.
```

8. Go to the hosted the **Dashboard** and click on **Policy**. Go to the **Cookbook** section on the hosted Chef instance and see if the **apt Cookbook** has been uploaded:

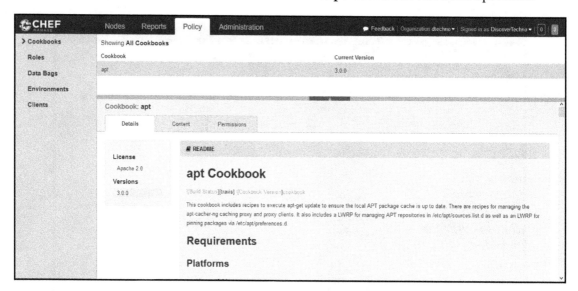

9. We need to upload all dependencies in terms of cookbooks for the Tomcat cookbook to be uploaded, otherwise it will give us an error. Upload all other cookbooks in order:

```
[root@devops1 chef-repo]# knife cookbook upload chef-sugar
Uploading chef-sugar     [3.3.0]
Uploaded 1 cookbook.
[root@devops1 chef-repo]# knife cookbook upload java
Uploading java           [1.39.0]
```

```
Uploaded 1 cookbook.
[root@devops1 chef-repo]# knife cookbook upload openssl
Uploading openssl        [4.4.0]
Uploaded 1 cookbook.
[root@devops1 chef-repo]# knife cookbook upload tomcat
Uploading tomcat         [0.17.0]
Uploaded 1 cookbook.
```

10. Go to the hosted Chef **Dashboard** and verify all the **Cookbooks**:

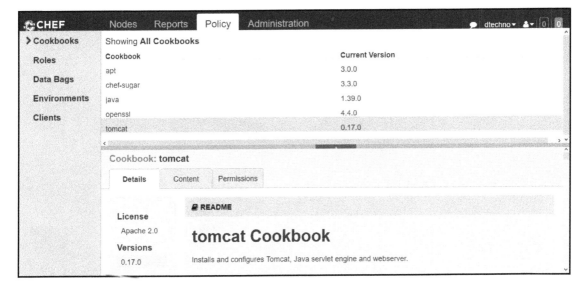

Once we have uploaded all the cookbooks to the hosted Chef, let's create a role.

Creating a role

At this stage, all the required cookbooks are uploaded on the hosted Chef. Now, let's create a role on the hosted Chef.

Before creating a role, let's understand what it means.

A role is created for a specific function. It provides a path for various patterns and workflow processes.

For example, the web server role can consist of Tomcat server recipes and any custom attributes:

1. Go to **Policy** in the hosted Chef **Dashboard** and click on **Roles** in the sidebar menu. Click on **Create Role** to create a role.
2. In the **Create Role** window, provide a **Name** and Description.
3. Click on **Next.**

Refer to the following screenshot:

1. A **Run List** keeps roles/recipes in a specific manner and order. It can be considered as the specifications of a node.
2. Select Tomcat from the **Available Recipes** list.
3. Drag the Tomcat recipe to the **Current Run List.**
4. Click on **Create Role.**

Refer to the following screenshot:

1. Check the newly added role in the hosted Chef **Dashboard** in the **Policy** tab:

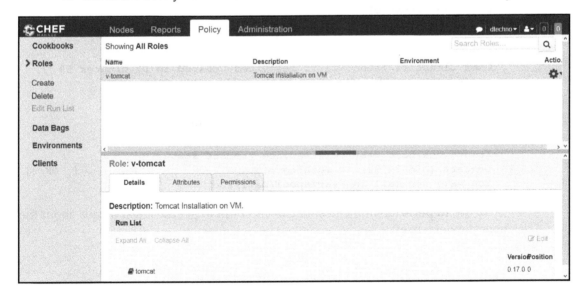

2. Now, let's specify a role while converging the node in the terminal. Add the role to the node with `knife node run_list add tomcatserver "role[v-tomcat]"`:

```
[root@devops1 chef-repo]# knife node run_list add
tomcatserver "role[v-tomcat]"
tomcatserver:
run_list: role[v-tomcat]
[root@devops1 chef-repo]#
```

3. The `v-tomcat` role is now being associated with the `tomcatserver` node.

4. Go to node and execute `chef-client`; it will execute the steps to bring the node status in compliance with the role assigned:

```
[root@localhost Desktop]# chef-client
Starting Chef Client, version 12.9.41
resolving cookbooks for run list: ["tomcat"]
Synchronizing Cookbooks:
    - tomcat (0.17.0)
    - chef-sugar (3.3.0)
    - java (1.39.0)
    - apt (3.0.0)
    - openssl (4.4.0)
Installing Cookbook Gems:
Compiling Cookbooks...
    .
    .
    .

Chef Client finished, 11/15 resources updated in 09 minutes 59
seconds
You have new mail in /var/spool/mail/root
```

5. Go to the node and check whether Tomcat is available or not:

```
[root@localhost Desktop]# service tomcat6 status
tomcat6 (pid 39782) is running...                          [  OK  ]
You have new mail in /var/spool/mail/root
```

6. Go to the **Reports** tab in the hosted Chef account to get the latest details about the node convergence:

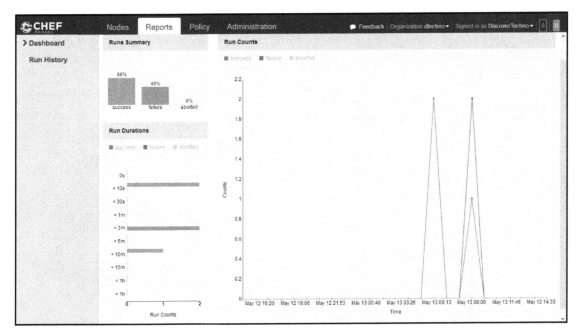

At this stage, we are ready with a hosted Chef account, configured workstation, and converged node.

In the next section, we will install knife plugins for some popular cloud platforms.

Installing knife plugins for Amazon Web Services and Microsoft Azure

Our objective is to install application packages to provide the runtime environment for our Java-based Petclinic application. In the traditional environment, we raise the acquisition request for the physical server and then the infrastructure team helps us to install different software on it to provide the runtime environment for our application. With Chef, we can install these packages using community cookbooks and hence we can automate it easily.

In this section, we will use cloud resources. Amazon EC2 and Microsoft Azure are two very popular public cloud resource providers. We will create virtual machines in the cloud environment and then install different application packages using the Chef configuration management tool:

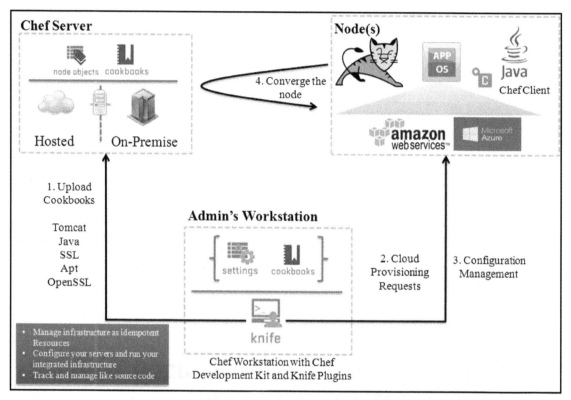

1. First, we will provision virtual machines in Amazon EC2 and Microsoft Azure using knife plugins using a Chef workstation.
2. Go to the Chef workstation.
3. Execute `knife` commands to create instances (Chef nodes) in Amazon EC2 and Microsoft Azure.

The following is how the process will work:

1. Execute the command on the Chef workstation to create a new instance in your cloud environment.
2. A new instance is created in Amazon EC2 and Microsoft Azure and it is up and running (the Chef node is available).
3. The Chef node communicates with the Chef server.

4. The Chef server instructs the Chef node to execute a list of tasks and download the Chef client.

5. A secure handshake takes place between the Chef server and the Chef node; the Chef server generates a security certificate that is used to authenticate the new node's upcoming queries.

6. The Chef node executes tasks and informs the Chef server regarding its compliance.

The following are the major benefits of using the Chef configuration management tool with different public cloud service providers as follows:

- Faster time to market
- Centralized control
- Standard policies
- Consistent environment to deploy the application
- Less or no manual effort and errors due to manual limitations
- Rapid application development
- Easy rollback
- High availability and disaster recovery for business continuity that is essential in today's day and age
- Community cookbooks accessible to all

The **Chef Development Kit** (**ChefDK**) provides development tools built by the Chef community that makes installing knife plugins easier.

Go to `https://downloads.chef.io/chef-dk/` and download ChefDK based on the operating system we use.

In our case, select Red Hat Enterprise Linux and select the ChefDK version. Click on Red Hat Enterprise Linux 6 and download it, as it works on 64-bit (`x86_64`) versions of Red Hat Enterprise Linux and CentOS 6:

```
[root@localhost Desktop]# sudo rpm -ivh chefdk-0.13.21-1.el6.x86_64.rpm
Preparing...                ###########################################
[100%]   1:chefdk
###########################################   [100%]
Thank you for installing Chef Development Kit!
```

Execute the `chef gem install knife-ec2` command to create, bootstrap, and manage Amazon EC2 instances. More details are available at `https://github.com/chef/knife-ec2`:

```
[root@localhost Desktop]# chef gem install knife-ec2
Fetching: knife-ec2-<version>.gem (100%)
.

.

Successfully installed knife-ec2-<version>
1 gem installed
```

Execute the `knife ec2 --help` command to check the available Amazon EC2 commands:

```
[root@localhost Desktop]# knife ec2 --help

** EC2 COMMANDS **
knife ec2 amis ubuntu DISTRO [TYPE] (options)
knife ec2 flavor list (options)
knife ec2 server create (options)
knife ec2 server delete SERVER [SERVER] (options)
knife ec2 server list (options)
```

Configure Amazon EC2 credentials for the `knife` plugin in the `knife.rb` file.

Use `knife[:aws_access_key_id]` and `knife[:aws_secret_access_key]` as shown here:

```
knife[:aws_access_key_id] = "Your AWS Access Key ID"
knife[:aws_secret_access_key] = "Your AWS Secret Access Key"
```

Execute the `chef gem install knife-azure` command to create, bootstrap, and manage Microsoft Azure virtual machines. More details are available at `https://github.com/chef/knife-ec2`:

```
[root@localhost Desktop]# chef gem install knife-azure -v 1.5.2
Fetching: knife-azure-1.5.2.gem (100%)

Successfully installed knife-azure-1.5.2
1 gem installed
```

Verify the available Azure commands using `knife azure --help`:

```
[root@localhost Desktop]# knife azure --help

** AZURE COMMANDS **
knife azure ag create (options)
knife azure ag list (options)
```

```
knife azure image list (options)
knife azure internal lb create (options)
knife azure internal lb list (options)
knife azure server create (options)
knife azure server delete SERVER [SERVER] (options)
knife azure server list (options)
knife azure server show SERVER [SERVER]
knife azure vnet create (options)
knife azure vnet list (options)
```

Creating and configuring a virtual machine in Amazon EC2

Use the `knife node list` command to get the list of nodes to get clarity on how many nodes are already configured using Chef:

```
root@devops1 Desktop]# knife node list
tomcatserver
```

Use the `knife ec2 server create` command with the following parameters to create a new virtual machine:

Parameter	Value	Description
-I	ami-1ecae776	This is the ID of the Amazon machine image
-f	t2.micro	This is the type of the virtual machine
-N	DevOpsVMonAWS	This is the name of the Chef node
--aws-access-key-id	Your access key ID	This is the access key ID of the AWS account
--aws-secret-access-key	Your secret access key	This is the secret access key of the AWS account
-S	Book	This is the SSH key
--identity-file	book.pem	This is the PEM file
--ssh-user	ec2-user	This is the user for the AWS instance
-r	role[v-tomcat]	This is the Chef role

Let's create an EC2 instance using the `knife` plugin:

```
[root@devops1 Desktop]# knife ec2 server create -I ami-1ecae776 -f t2.micro
-N DevOpsVMonAWS --aws-access-key-id '< Your Access Key ID >' --aws-secret-
access-key '< Your Secret Access Key >' -S book --identity-file book.pem --
ssh-user ec2-user -r role[v-tomcat]

Instance ID: i-640d2de3
Flavor: t2.micro
Image: ami-1ecae776
Region: us-east-1
Availability Zone: us-east-1a
Security Groups: default
Tags: Name: DevOpsVMonAWS
SSH Key: book

Waiting for EC2 to create the instance......
Public DNS Name: ******************.compute-1.amazonaws.com
Public IP Address: **.**.***.***
Private DNS Name: ip-***-**-1-27.ec2.internal
Private IP Address: ***.**.*.27
```

At this stage, the AWS EC2 instance has been created and is `Waiting for sshd access to become available`:

```
Waiting for sshd access to become available...................done

Creating new client for DevOpsVMonAWS
Creating new node for DevOpsVMonAWS
Connecting to ec2-**-**-***-***.compute-1.amazonaws.com

ec2-**-**-***-***.compute-1.amazonaws.com -----> Installing Chef Omnibus (-
v 12)
  .

  .
ec2-**-**-***-***.compute-1.amazonaws.com version12.9.41
ec2-**-**-***-***.compute-1.amazonaws.com downloaded metadata file looks
valid...
ec2-**-**-***-***.compute-1.amazonaws.com downloading
https://packages.chef.io/stable/el/6/chef-12.9.41-1.el6.x86_64.rpm
ec2-**-**-***-***.compute-1.amazonaws.com
1:chef-12.9.41-1.el6              ############################## [100%]

ec2-**-**-***-***.compute-1.amazonaws.com Thank you for installing Chef!
```

Now, the Chef client has been installed on the AWS instance. It is ready for the initial `Chef Client run` with `version 12.9.41`:

```
ec2-**-**-***-***.compute-1.amazonaws.com Starting the first Chef Client
run...
ec2-**-**-***-***.compute-1.amazonaws.com Starting Chef Client, version
12.9.41
```

It is now ready to resolve cookbooks based on the role and install runtime environments:

```
ec2-**-**-***-***.compute-1.amazonaws.com resolving cookbooks for run list:
["tomcat"]
ec2-**-**-***-***.compute-1.amazonaws.com Synchronizing Cookbooks:
ec2-**-**-***-***.compute-1.amazonaws.com  - tomcat (0.17.0)
ec2-**-**-***-***.compute-1.amazonaws.com  - java (1.39.0)
ec2-**-**-***-***.compute-1.amazonaws.com  - apt (3.0.0)
ec2-**-**-***-***.compute-1.amazonaws.com  - openssl (4.4.0)
ec2-**-**-***-***.compute-1.amazonaws.com  - chef-sugar (3.3.0)

ec2-**-**-***-***.compute-1.amazonaws.com Installing Cookbook Gems:
ec2-**-**-***-***.compute-1.amazonaws.com Compiling Cookbooks...

ec2-**-**-***-***.compute-1.amazonaws.com Converging 3 resources
ec2-**-**-***-***.compute-1.amazonaws.com Recipe: tomcat::default
ec2-**-**-***-***.compute-1.amazonaws.com   * yum_package[tomcat6] action
install
ec2-**-**-***-***.compute-1.amazonaws.com      - install version
6.0.45-1.4.amzn1 of package tomcat6
ec2-**-**-***-***.compute-1.amazonaws.com   * yum_package[tomcat6-admin-
webapps] action install
ec2-**-**-***-***.compute-1.amazonaws.com      - install version
6.0.45-1.4.amzn1 of package tomcat6-admin-webapps
ec2-**-**-***-***.compute-1.amazonaws.com   * tomcat_instance[base] action
configure (up to date)
```

The runtime environment is available now and it is time to start Tomcat services in the AWS instance; verify the logs:

```
ec2-**-**-***-***.compute-1.amazonaws.com
ec2-**-**-***-***.compute-1.amazonaws.com   * service[tomcat6] action start
.

.
ec2-**-**-***-***.compute-1.amazonaws.com Chef Client finished, 13/15
resources updated in 01 minutes 13 seconds
```

Here are the details of the newly created AWS instance:

```
Instance ID: i-********
Flavor: t2.micro
Image: ami-1ecae776
Region: us-****-1
Availability Zone: us-****-1a
Security Groups: default
Security Group Ids: default
Tags: Name: DevOpsVMonAWS
SSH Key: book
Root Device Type: ebs
Root Volume ID: vol-1e0e83b5
Root Device Name: /dev/xvda
Root Device Delete on Terminate: true
Public DNS Name: ec2-**-**-***-***.compute-1.amazonaws.com
Public IP Address: 52.90.219.205
Private DNS Name: ip-172-31-1-27.ec2.internal
Private IP Address: 172.31.1.27
Environment: _default
Run List: role[v-tomcat]
You have new mail in /var/spool/mail/root
[root@devops1 Desktop]#
```

Go to https://aws.amazon.com/ and sign in.

Go to the **Amazon EC2** section and click on **Instances** in the left-hand sidebar or on **Running Instances** on the **Resources** page get to the details about AWS instances.

Verify the **Name**, **Tags**, **Public DNS**, and other details that we get in the Chef client run with the details available on the Amazon **Dashboard**:

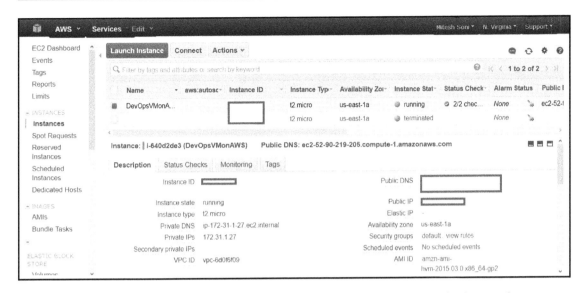

Now, let's go to the hosted Chef **Dashboard** and click on **Nodes** to verify the newly created/converged node in Amazon EC2:

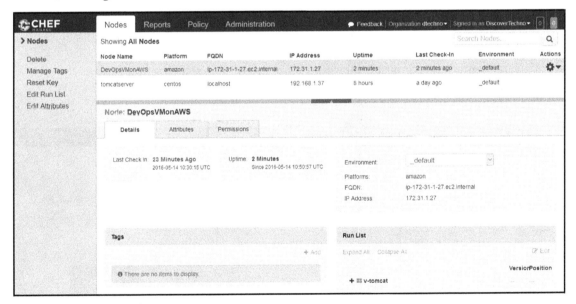

Verify the instance **Details** and **Run List**:

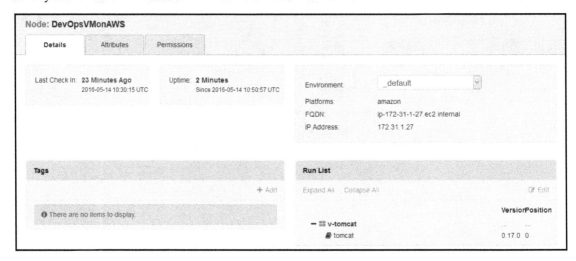

An instance is created in Amazon EC2 and Tomcat is also installed and its service is also started, we can verify whether it is actually running or not.

Let's try to access the Tomcat server installed on the AWS instance using the public domain name of the instance:

1. If it gives the connection has timed out error, then the reason for this is the restriction of security groups in AWS. Go to the **Security Group** in the AWS instance:

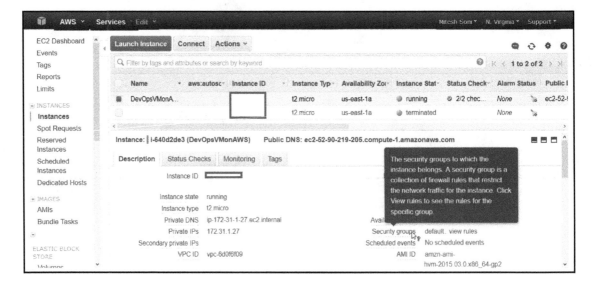

2. In the **AWS** portal, go to the **Security Group** section. Select the default security group to verify the inbound rules. We can see only the **SSH** rule available; we need to allow port 8080 so that we can access it:

3. Let's create a new custom rule with port **8080**:

4. Now, try to access the public domain URL, and we will get the Tomcat page on our AWS instance.

In the next section, we will create and configure a virtual machine in Microsoft Azure.

Creating and configuring a virtual machine in Microsoft Azure

To create and configure Chef and Microsoft Azure integration, we need to provide the Microsoft Azure account and credentials. To get Microsoft Azure credentials, download the `publishsettings` file and perform the following steps:

1. Login to the Microsoft Azure portal using the login name and password and download a `publishsettings` file from `https://manage.windowsazure.com/publishsettings/index?client=xplat`.

2. Copy it on a Chef workstation and refer to this local file by creating an entry in the `knife.rb` file:

```
knife[:azure_publish_settings_file] = "~/<name>.publishsettings"
```

3. The following are the parameters to create a virtual machine in the Microsoft Azure public cloud:

Parameter	Value	Description
--azure-dns-name	distechnodemo	This is the DNS name
--azure-vm-name	dtserver02	This is the name of the virtual machine
--azure-vm-size	Small	This is the size of the virtual machine
-N	DevOpsVMonAzure2	This is the name of the Chef node
--azure-storage-account	classicstorage9883	This is Azure's storage account

`--bootstrap-protocol`	cloud-api	This is the Bootstrap protocol
`--azure-source-image`	5112500ae3b842c8b9c604889f8753c3__OpenLogic-CentOS-67-20160310	This is the name of the Azure source image
`--azure-service-location`	Central US	This is the Azure location to host the virtual machine
`--ssh-user`	dtechno	This is the SSH user
`--ssh-password`	<YOUR PASSWORD>	This is the SSH password
`-r`	role[v-tomcat]	This is the role
`--ssh-port`	22	This is the SSH port

We have installed the `knife azure` plugin successfully. Now we can create the virtual machine in Microsoft Azure Cloud by executing the `knife azure server create` command as follows:

```
[root@devops1 Desktop]# knife azure server create --azure-dns-name
'distechnodemo' --azure-vm-name 'dtserver02' --azure-vm-size 'Small' -N
DevOpsVMonAzure2 --azure-storage-account 'classicstorage9883' --bootstrap-
protocol 'cloud-api' --azure-source-image
'5112500ae3b842c8b9c604889f8753c3__OpenLogic-CentOS-67-20160310' --azure-
service-location 'Central US' --ssh-user 'dtechno' --ssh-password
'cloud@321' -r role[v-tomcat] --ssh-port 22
.
.
.
Creating new node for DevOpsVMonAzure2
.........
Waiting for virtual machine to reach status 'provisioning'.............vm
state 'provisioning' reached after 2.47 minutes.
..

DNS Name: distechnodemo.cloudapp.net
VM Name: dtserver02
Size: Small
Azure Source Image: 5112500ae3b842c8b9c604889f8753c3__OpenLogic-
```

```
CentOS-67-20160310
Azure Service Location: Central US
Private Ip Address: 100.73.210.70
Environment: _default

Runlist: ["role[v-tomcat]"]
```

Now we will start with resource provisioning in Microsoft Azure Public Cloud:

```
Waiting for Resource Extension to reach status 'wagent
provisioning'.....Resource extension state 'wagent provisioning' reached
after 0.17 minutes.

Waiting for Resource Extension to reach status
'installing'...................Resource extension state 'installing'
reached after 2.21 minutes.
Waiting for Resource Extension to reach status 'provisioning'.....Resource
extension state 'provisioning' reached after 0.19 minutes.
..
DNS Name: distechnodemo.cloudapp.net
VM Name: dtserver02
Size: Small
Azure Source Image: 5112500ae3b842c8b9c604889f8753c3__OpenLogic-
CentOS-67-20160310
Azure Service Location: Central US
Private Ip Address: 100.73.210.70
Environment: _default
Runlist: ["role[v-tomcat]"]
[root@devops1 Desktop]#
```

1. Go to the hosted Chef account in the browser and click on the **Nodes** tab.
2. Verify that the new node we created on Microsoft Azure Public Cloud has been registered on the hosted Chef server.
3. We can see the DevOpsVMonAzure2 **Node Name**:

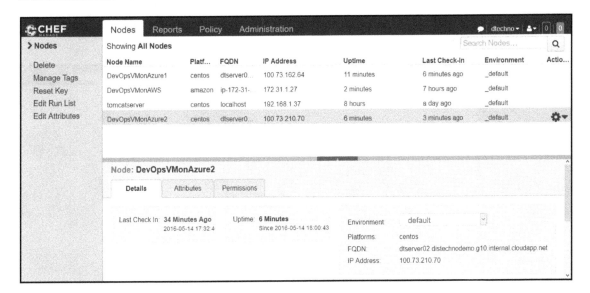

4. Go to the **Microsoft Azure** portal and click on the **VIRTUAL MACHINES** section to verify the newly created virtual machine using the Chef configuration management tool:

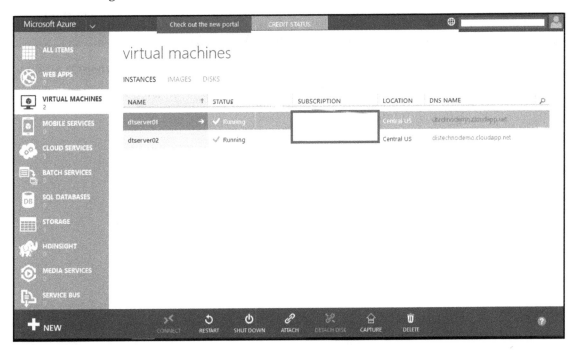

5. Click on **VIRTUAL MACHINES** in the **Microsoft Azure Dashboard**, and verify the details of virtual machines:

6. Go to the bottom of the **virtual machines** page, and verify the **extensions** section.
7. Check whether it shows **chef-service enabled**:

We have now created virtual machines in Amazon EC2 and Microsoft Azure using `knife` plugins with installed runtime environment using role.

Summary

In this chapter, we installed and configured a Chef workstation, we converged the node, created a role, and installed the runtime environment for Java-based web applications. We also used `knife` plugins to create virtual machines in Microsoft Azure and Amazon EC2 and used a role to install a runtime environment.

In the next chapter, we will see how to deploy Java-based web applications into the web server in an automated way using scripts or plugins.

We will deploy our WAR file into the local or remote Tomcat. The remote Tomcat will be on Amazon EC2, Microsoft Azure Virtual Machine, AWS Elastic Beanstalk, or Microsoft Azure Web Apps.

5
Continuous Delivery

Technology is nothing. What's important is that you have a faith in people, that they're basically good and smart, and if you give them tools, they'll do wonderful things with them
- Steve Jobs

We have looked at different DevOps practices such as continuous integration, containers, and configuration management. Now we will look at how to deploy a package file in to a web container or web server. We will use Apache Tomcat as a web server in cloud virtual machines to deploy our Java-based application.

The main objective of this chapter is to make you the reader aware of different ways to deploy an application package into a web server. These ways can be utilized based on the access available to the team and, once we achieve this automated delivery into the web server, then we can utilize this operation in the overall build orchestration.

So, we can create a build pipeline and this orchestration will help us to achieve continuous delivery and continuous deployment.

In this chapter, we are going to cover the following topics:

- Continuous delivery in Docker container using Jenkins plugin
- Continuous delivery in AWS EC2 and Microsoft Azure VM using script
- Continuous delivery in AWS Elastic Beanstalk using a Jenkins plugin
- Continuous delivery in Microsoft Azure App Services using FTP
- Continuous delivery in Microsoft Azure App Services using VSTS

Continuous delivery in Docker container using Jenkins Plugin

Let's understand how we can deploy a web application in Tomcat using the Jenkins plugin.

We can follow a few steps for that:

- Run Apache Tomcat
- Use the proper IP address and port number combination to navigate to the Tomcat home page:

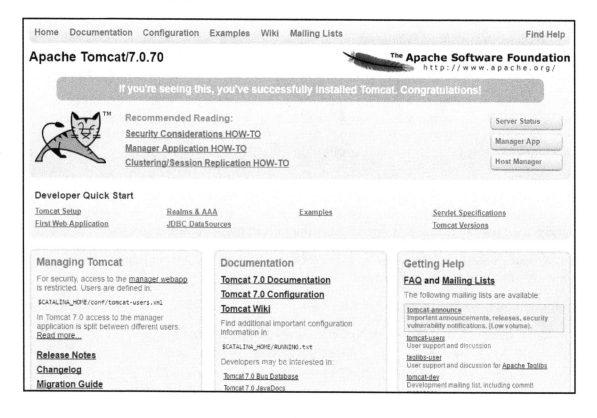

- Go to the `conf` directory and then open `tomcat-users.xml` in your Tomcat installation directory and un-comment the role and user lines or rewrite them. Set **manager-script** as the **rolename** for testing purposes. We need **manager-script** for deployment via the `Deploy to Container` plugin.
- For the Jenkins deploy plugin, change the **rolename** to **manager-script** as follows:

```xml
<?xml version='1.0' encoding='utf-8'?>
<!--
<tomcat-users>
<!--
<!--
    NOTE:  The sample user and role entries below are intended for use with the
    examples web application. They are wrapped in a comment and thus are ignored
    when reading this file. If you wish to configure these users for use with the
    examples web application, do not forget to remove the <!.. ..> that surrounds
    them. You will also need to set the passwords to something appropriate.
-->
    <role rolename="manager-script"/>
    <user username="admin" password="admin@123" roles="manager-script"/>
</tomcat-users>
```

- Click on the manager application link on the Tomcat home page and enter the username and password you set in `tomcat-users.xml`. Now we can access the management application. For a local Tomcat, we can use localhost to access the Tomcat page or we can use the IP address as well. For a remote web server, we can utilize an IP address or domain name to access Tomcat.
- Restart Tomcat and visit `https://<IP Address>:8080/manager/text/list`. You should see this output:

```
OK - Listed applications for virtual host localhost
/:running:0:ROOT
/petclinic:running:1:petclinic
/examples:running:0:examples
/host-manager:running:0:host-manager
/manager:running:0:manager
/docs:running:0:docs
```

- Go to the **Jenkins** job build page and click on **Configure**. Select the proper **JDK** configuration for the Jenkins agent:

- Under **Post-build Actions**, select **Deploy war/ear to a container**. Provide the location of the WAR file in the Jenkins workspace, the Tomcat manager credentials, and the **Tomcat URL** with the port:

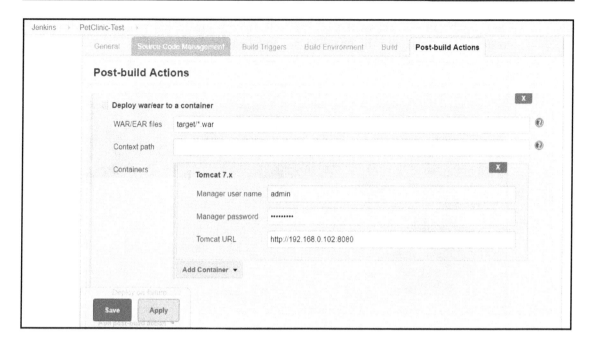

- Click on **Apply** and **Save**. Click on **Build now** on the **Jenkins** build's page. Verify that the console output is showing a fresh deployment:

```
Results :

Tests run: 59, Failures: 0, Errors: 0, Skipped: 0

[INFO]
[INFO] --- maven-war-plugin:2.3:war (default-war) @ spring-petclinic ---
[INFO] Packaging webapp
[INFO] Assembling webapp [spring-petclinic] in [d:\jenkins\workspace\PetClinic-Test\target\spring-
petclinic-4.2.5-SNAPSHOT]
[INFO] Processing war project
[INFO] Copying webapp resources [d:\jenkins\workspace\PetClinic-Test\src\main\webapp]
[INFO] Webapp assembled in [1669 msecs]
[INFO] Building war: d:\jenkins\workspace\PetClinic-Test\target\spring-petclinic-4.2.5-SNAPSHOT.war
[INFO] ------------------------------------------------------------------------
[INFO] BUILD SUCCESS
[INFO] ------------------------------------------------------------------------
[INFO] Total time: 28.772 s
[INFO] Finished at: 2016-07-06T22:59:37+05:30
[INFO] Final Memory: 29M/261M
[INFO] ------------------------------------------------------------------------
Deploying d:\jenkins\workspace\PetClinic-Test\target\spring-petclinic-4.2.5-SNAPSHOT.war to container
Tomcat 7.x Remote
  [d:\jenkins\workspace\PetClinic-Test\target\spring-petclinic-4.2.5-SNAPSHOT.war] is not deployed.
Doing a fresh deployment.
  Deploying [d:\jenkins\workspace\PetClinic-Test\target\spring-petclinic-4.2.5-SNAPSHOT.war]
Finished: SUCCESS
```

- Once the build is successful, visit the URL from your browser and notice the context. It is similar to the name of the application:

We already know the basic operations available in Docker, as we covered them in Chapter 3, *Containers*. We have created a customized Tomcat image with tomcat-users.xml.

Once Docker is up and running, we are ready to create a Docker container. Note the IP address of the default Docker machine in the following image:

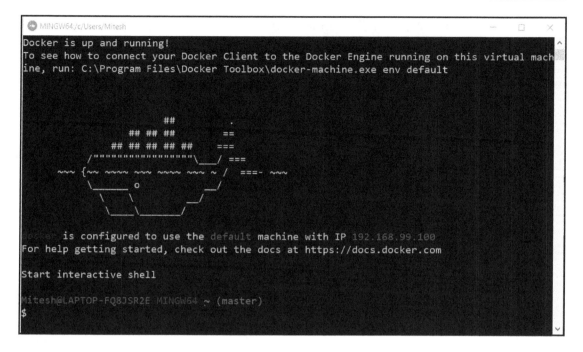

- To change the name of the container, use :

```
docker run -it -p 9999:8080 --name bootcamp_tomcat
devops_tomcat_sc
```

- Verify the name using :

```
dockerps -a
```

- Use the virtual machine IP address and use **9999** as a port number to access Tomcat running in the container:

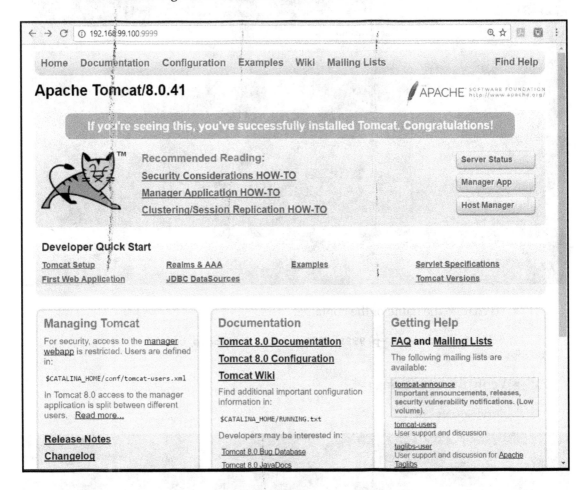

- Verify the manager access with the `manager-script` role using the following URL:

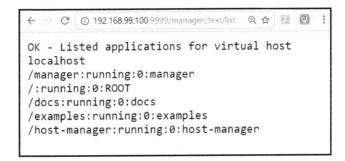

- Let's just try to deploy an application using the `Deploy to Container` plugin in Tomcat. If one build job generates a WAR file, then copy it from that build using the **copy artifact** plugin:

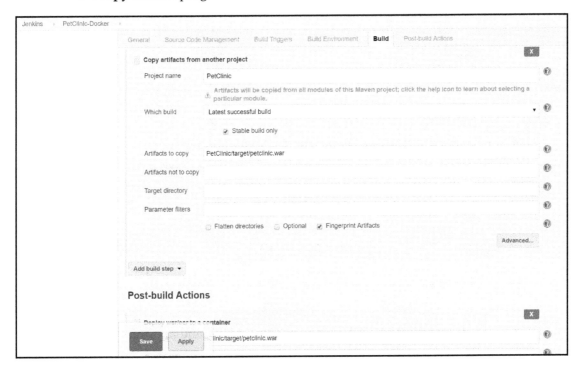

- In **Post-build actions**, select **Deploy war/ear to a container**. Give the user name and password provided in `tomcat-users.xml`. We will then provide the **Tomcat URL**, shown as follows. After filling in the details , click on **Apply/Save**:

- Click on **Build Now**.

- Go to console output and verify the deployment process:

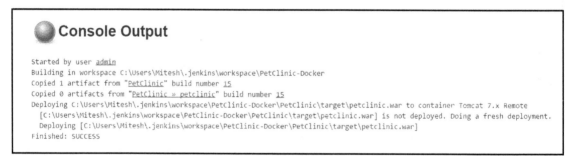

- Verify the application URL using the Tomcat URL and application context.

Awesome!! We have successfully created an image and a container, and deployed the application in the Tomcat container.

Continuous Delivery in AWS EC2 and Microsoft Azure VM using Script

We have already created VMs in AWS and Microsoft Azure in Chapter 4, *Cloud Computing and Configuration Management*. To deploy an application in AWS and Microsoft Azure VM, we need a WAR package file. Once it is created by the Jenkins build job, we need to perform the following steps:

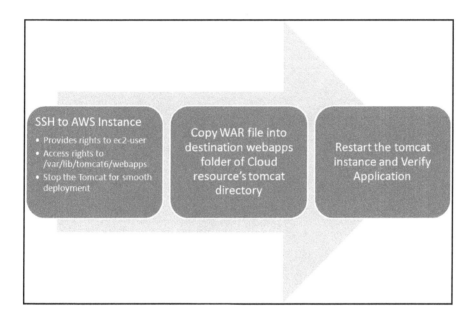

Let's configure the build job to execute the deployment of the **WAR** file in the AWS instance by executing the commands shown as follows:

- Give rights to ec2-user in the webapps directory of Tomcat so we can copy the WAR file:

```
ssh -i /home/mitesh/book.pem -o StrictHostKeyChecking=no -t -t
ec2-user@ec2-52-90-116-36.compute-1.amazonaws.com "sudousermod -a
-G tomcat ec2-user;
sudochmod -R g+w /var/lib/tomcat6/webapps; sudo service tomcat6
stop;"
```

- Copy the WAR file into the remote directory:

```
scp -i /home/mitesh/book.pem /home/mitesh/target/*.war ec2-
user@ec2-52-90-116-36.compute-
1.amazonaws.com:/var/lib/tomcat6/webapps
```

- Start/restart the Tomcat service:

```
ssh -i /home/mitesh/book.pem -o StrictHostKeyChecking=no -t -t
ec2-user@ec2-52-90-116-36.compute-1.amazonaws.com "sudo service
tomcat6 start"
```

Use the `Copy Artifact` plugin to copy the **WAR** file from another build job and then execute the preceding commands in **Execute Shell Build Actions**:

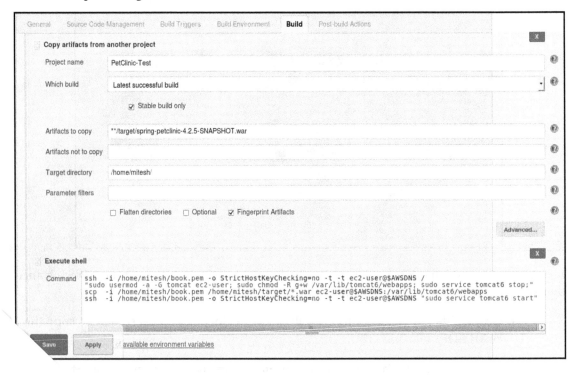

Click on **Save** and then execute the build job. For application deployment in Microsoft Azure VM, utilize Jenkins plugin (**Deploy to Container**) or script utilized for AWS with required modification as self exercise.

Continuous delivery in AWS Elastic Beanstalk using Jenkins Plugin

AWS Elastic Beanstalk is a **Platform as a Service(PaaS)** offering from Amazon. We will use it to deploy the PetClinic application on the AWS platform. The good part is we don't need to manage the infrastructure or even the platform, as it is a PaaS offering. We can configure scaling and other details. These are the steps to deploy an application on AWS Elastic Beanstalk:

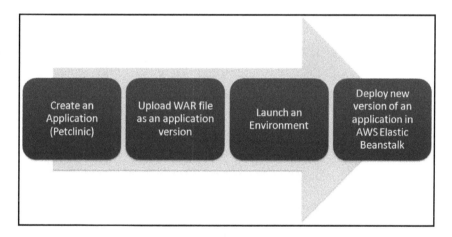

Let's create a sample application to understand how Elastic Beanstalk works and then use the `Jenkins` plugin to deploy an application.

- Go to the AWS management console and verify whether we have a default **Virtual Private Cloud** (**VPC**). If you've deleted the default VPC and subnet by accident, send a request to AWS customer support to recreate it:

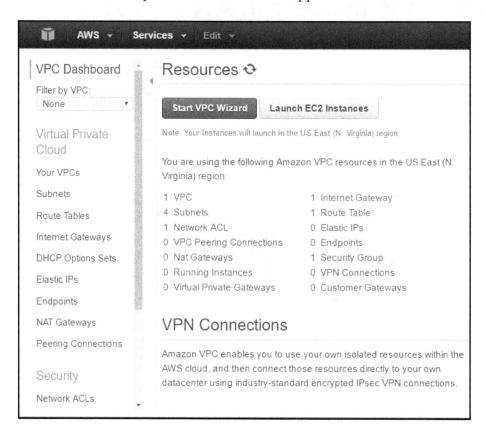

- Click on **Services** in the AWS management console and select AWS **Elastic Beanstalk**. Create a new application named **petclinic**. Select **Tomcat** as a **Platform** and select the **Sample application** radio button:

- Verify the sequence of events for the creation of a sample application:

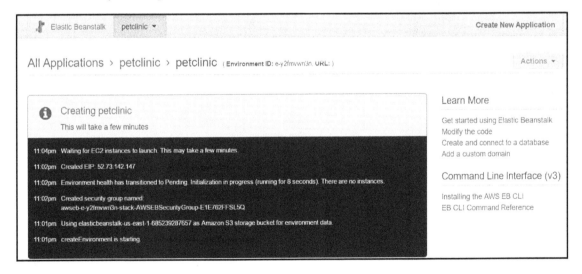

- It will take a while, and once the environment has been created, it will be highlighted in green, as shown here:

- Click on the **petclinic** environment and verify **Health** and **Running Version** in the dashboard:

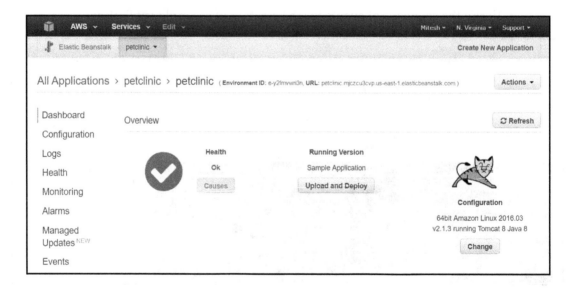

- Verify the environment ID and URL. Click on the **URL** and verify the default page:

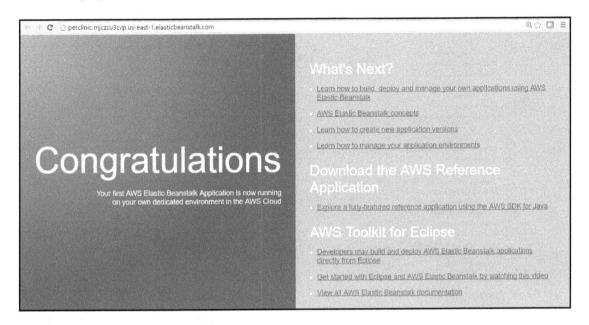

- Install the AWS Elastic Beanstalk `Publisher` plugin.

For more details, visit `https://wiki.jenkins-ci.org/display/JENKINS` `/AWS+Beanstalk+Publisher+Plugin`.

- Open the Jenkins dashboard and go to **Build** job. Click on **Post-build Actions** and select **Deploy into AWS Elastic Beanstalk**:

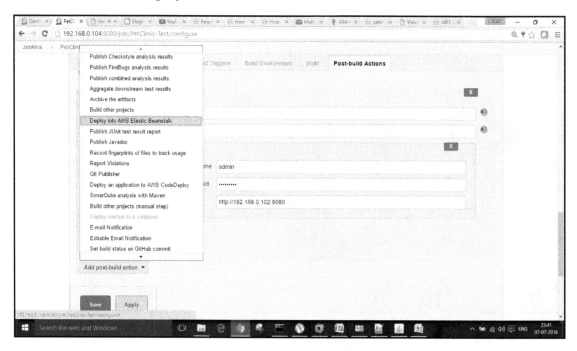

- A new section will come up in **Post-build Actions** for **Elastic Beanstalk**.
- Click on the **Jenkins** dashboard and select **Credentials**; add your AWS credentials.
- Go to your Jenkins build and select **AWS Credential**, which is set in the global configuration.
- Select **AWS Region** from the list and click on **Get Available Applications**. As we have created a sample application, it will show up like this.
- In **EnvironmentLookup**, provide an environment ID in the **Get Environments By Name** box and click on **Get Available Environments**:

- Save the configuration and click on **Build now**.

Now let's verify the AWS management console to check whether the **WAR** file is being copied in Amazon S3 or not:

- Go to S3 Services and check the available buckets:

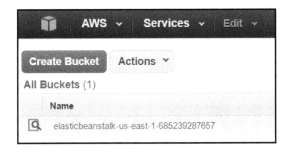

- Since the WAR file is large, it will take a while to upload to Amazon S3. Once it is uploaded, it will be available in the Amazon S3 bucket.

- Verify the build job's execution status in Jenkins. Some sections of the expected output are that:
  - The test case execution and WAR file creation are successful
  - The build is successful
- Now check the AWS management console:

- Go to **Services**, click on AWS **Elastic Beanstalk**, and verify the environment. The previous version was Sample Application. Now, the version is updated as given in **Version Label Format** in the Jenkins build job configuration:

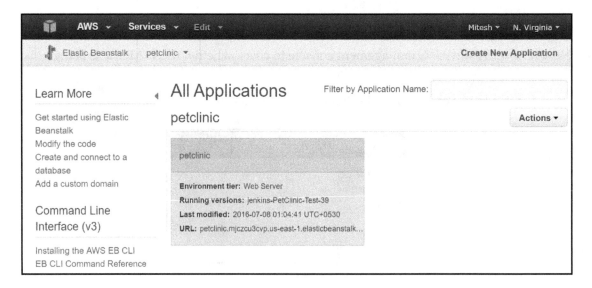

- Go to the dashboard and verify **Health** and **Running Version** again.
- Once everything has been verified, click on the URL for the environment, and our PetClinic application is live:

- Once the application deployment is successful, terminate the environment:

We have thus successfully deployed our application on Elastic Beanstalk.

Continuous delivery in Microsoft Azure App Services Using FTP

Microsoft Azure app services is a PaaS. In this section, we will look at the Azure Web App and how we can deploy our PetClinic application.

Let's install the `Publish Over FTP` plugin in Jenkins. We will use the Azure Web App's FTP details to publish the PetClinic WAR file:

- Go to the Microsoft Azure portal at `https://portal.azure.com`. Click on **App Services** and then on **Add**. Provide values for **App Name**, **Subscription**, **Resource Group**, and **App Service plan/Location**. Click on **Create**:

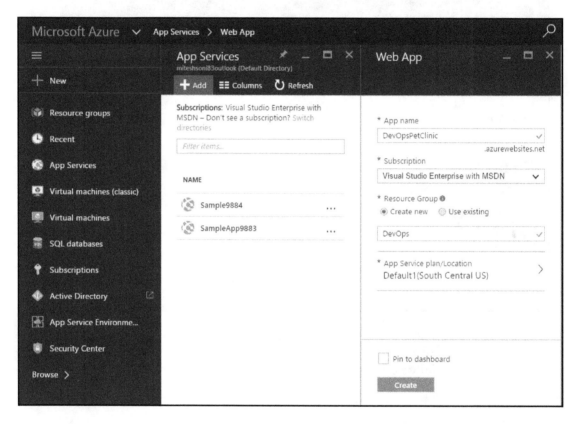

- Once the Azure Web App is created, see whether it shows up in the Azure portal.
- Click on **DevOpsPetClinic** in details related to the **URL**, **Status**, **Location**, and so on:

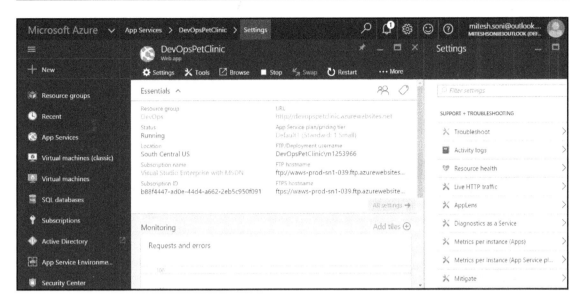

- Click on **All Settings**, go to the **GENERAL** section and click on **Application settings** to configure the Azure Web App for Java web application hosting. Select the **Java version**, **Java Minor version**, **Web container**, and **Platform**, and click on **Always On**:

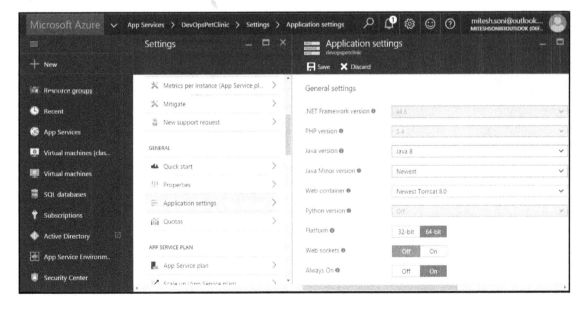

- Visit the URL of an Azure Web App from your browser and verify that it is ready for hosting our sample spring application, PetClinic:

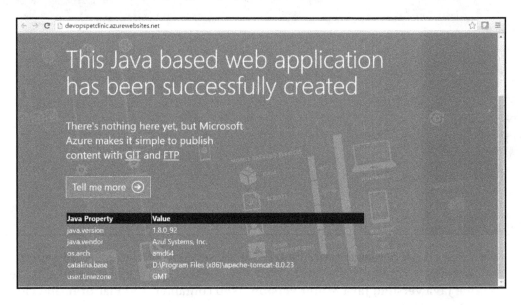

- Let's go to the **Jenkins** dashboard. Click on **New Item** and select **Freestyle project**.
- Click on **All Settings**, and go to **Deployment credentials** in the **PUBLISHING** section. Provide a username and password, and save your changes:

- In Jenkins, go to **Manage Jenkins** and click on **Configure | Configure FTP** settings. Provide a **Hostname**, **Username**, and **Password**, available in the Azure portal.

- Go to `devopspetclinic.scm.azurewebsites.net` and download the Kudu console. Navigate to the different options and find the `site directory` and `webapps` directory.

- Click on **Test Configuration** and, once you get a **Success** message, you are ready to deploy the PetClinic application:

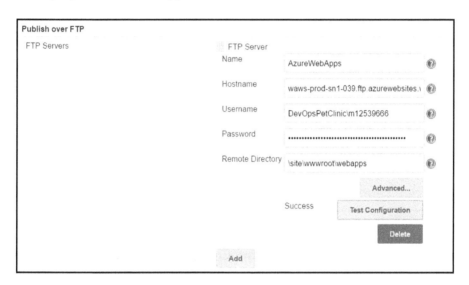

- In the build job we created, go to the **Build** section and configure **Copy artifacts from another project**. We will copy the WAR file to a specific location on a virtual machine:

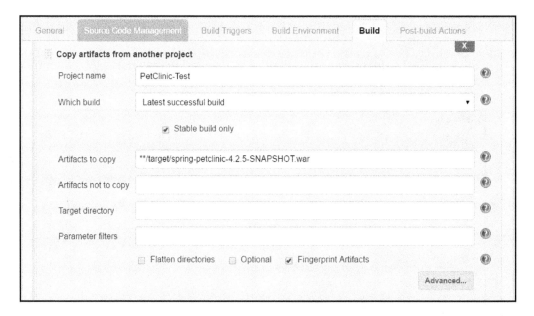

- In **Post-build Actions**, click on **Send build artifacts over FTP**. Select the **FTP Server Name** configured in Jenkins. Configure **Source files** and the **Remove prefix** accordingly for deployment of an Azure Web App:
- Tick **Verbose output in console**:

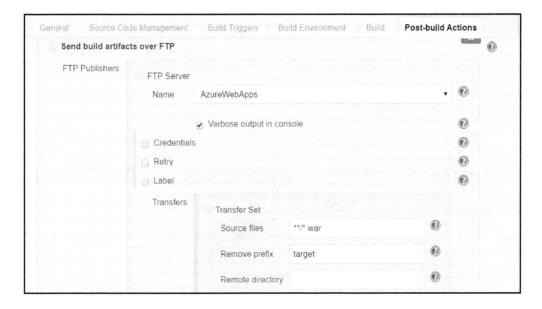

- Click on **Build now** and see what happens behind the scenes:
- Go to the **Kudu** console, click on **DebugConsole**, and go to **Powershell**. Go to **site | wwwroot | webapps**. Check whether the WAR file has been copied:
- Visit the Azure Web App URL in the browser with the context of an application:

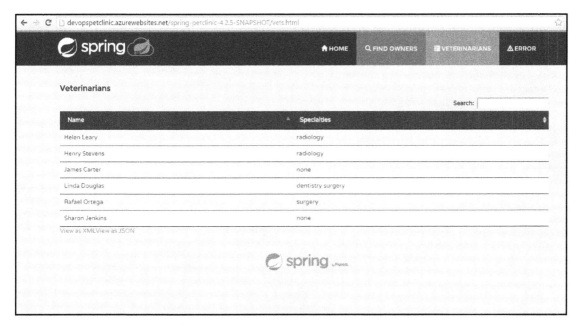

Now we have an application deployed on Azure Web Apps.

It is important to note that the FTP username has to be with the domain. In our case, it can be `Sample9888\m1253966`. Using the username without the web app name won't work.

All these different ways of deploying to AWS IaaS, AWS PaaS, Microsoft Azure PaaS, and Docker container can be used in the final end-to-end automation.

Continuous delivery in Microsoft Azure App Services Using VSTS

Visual Studio Team Services provides a way to configure continuous integration and continuous delivery. We will first go to our VSTS account. Here, we need the following things to be accomplished:

- Configure Microsoft Azure Subscription so we can connect to Azure Web Apps from VSTS
- Create a release definition that achieves the task of application deployment in Azure Web Apps

In the **Recent projects & teams**, click on **PetClinic**:

It will open a **Home** page for the project created in VSTS:

In the top menu bar, click on **Build & Release**, which will open a menu. Click on the **Releases** menu item from it:

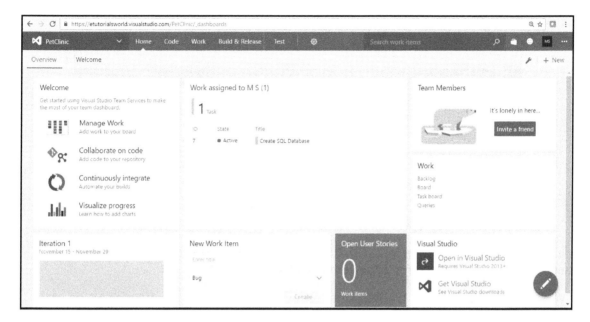

Click on the **Releases** link on the page.

As this is the new account, there is no Release definition created that has been created yet, so this section is empty. We can create a **New Release** definition so we can automate application deployment into Azure App Services or the App Service Environment.

In the same way that we have built definition for continuous integration, we have release definition for continuous release or continuous delivery or continuous deployment. Release definition contains different tasks that can be used for application deployment in the target environment. Each release definition contains one or more environments, and each environment contains one or more tasks to deploy the application.

So, let's create a new release definition. Each release definition can contain one or more environment and each environment can contain one or more tasks to deploy an application.

Click on **New definition**:

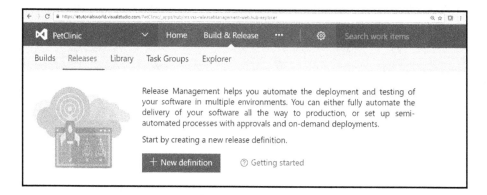

Once we click on the new release definition, it will open a dialog box with deployment templates that can be used for deployment automation.

We are going to deploy the WAR file into Azure App Service / Azure Web Apps, so select **Azure App Service Deployment**.

Click on **Next**:

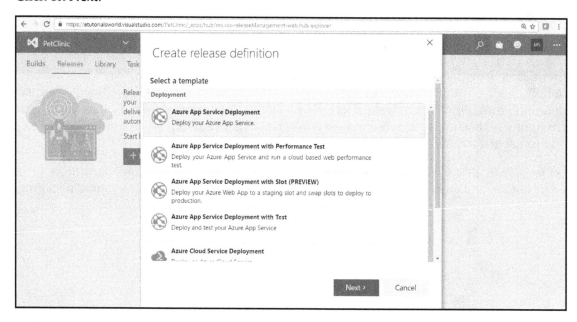

Let's review a few things from earlier chapters before explaining this deployment automation.

We created a build definition **PetClinic-Maven** that compiles the source code, executes unit test cases and creates a WAR file. WAR file is our artifact. This artifact is the result of the build definition execution.

Now, in the release definition, we need to select where the artifact will come from, and that is from **Build**.

Select the **PetClinic** project.

In **Source (Build definition)**, all build definitions related to the **PetClinic** project will be available. We will select **PetClinic-Maven**.

In a nutshell, we want to achieve continuous integration and continuous delivery here. It means that, when a developer checks any new code or bug fix in the repository, it will automatically trigger a build definition. Build definition will compile source files, execute unit tests, if any, conduct a static code analysis if sonar is configured, and create a WAR/package file. That is an artifact. Once build definition has completed successfully, it will trigger a release definition to deploy an artifact or a **WAR** file into Azure Web Apps that is hosted in an ASE or a non-ASE environment.

Click on the **Continuous deployment (create release and deploy whenever a build completes)** checkbox.

Click on **Create**:

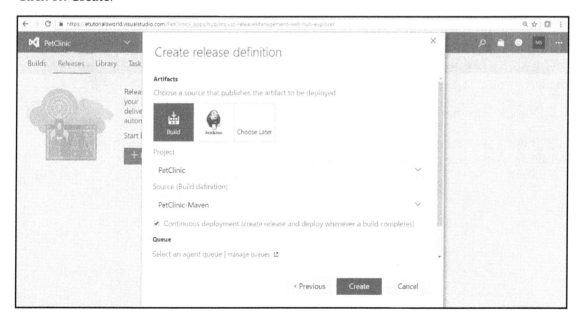

This will open a release definition in the edit mode. We selected **Deploy Azure App Service**. The first thing that is required is to configure an Azure subscription with VSTS.

Click on the **task** and see there are two fields named **AzureRM Subscription** and **App Service Name**. We need to configure Azure subscription here and **App Service Name** will come in the list automatically.

Click on **Manage** link next to the **AzureRM Subscription** field:

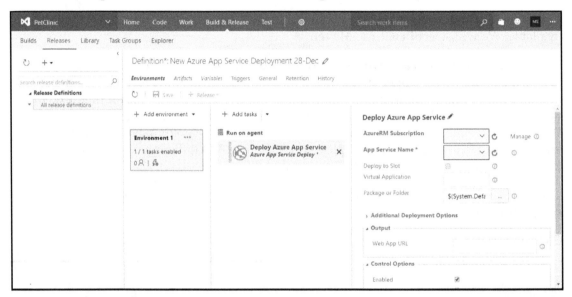

It will open a **Services** page in the VSTS portal. As of now, there is no service configured, so the list is empty:

Click on the **New Service Endpoint**.

It will open a menu; select the **Azure Resource Manager** menu item from the menu to configure Azure subscription:

As we are already logged into VSTS and our Azure account, it will show the subscription name in the list. In **Connection name**, give the name that we will use in the release definition task to connect to our Azure Account.

Click on **OK**.

The purpose of adding the Azure subscription here is to get a list of resources available in that subscription to VSTS so that we can configure them for deployment. In our example, we need a list of Azure Web Apps that are hosted in ASE or non-ASE so we can deploy the PetClinic application to Azure Web Apps.

Once we close the box to add an **Azure RM Endpoint**, we can see a list of endpoints in services.

Hence, we have Azure RM subscription configured successfully:

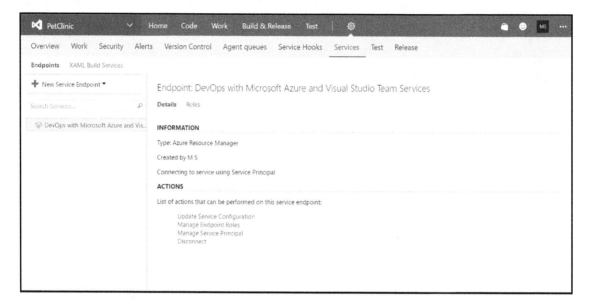

Click on the **Roles** link to verify the available roles of the Azure subscription:

Now go to **Release Definitions** and click on the list box of **AzureRM Subscription**, and now our newly added **Endpoint** is available in the list.

Select **Endpoint**:

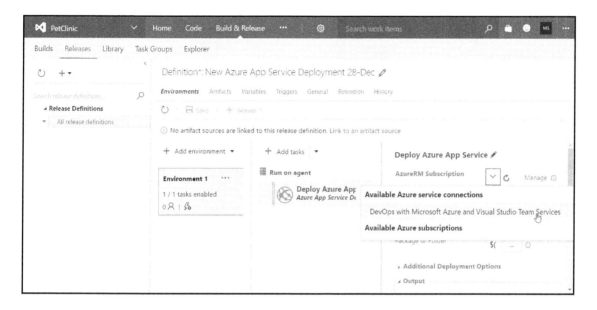

So far, we have configured Azure Subscription Endpoint in VSTS so we can use it in **Release Definition**s to deploy the artifact in Azure App Services hosted in ASE and non-ASE environments. We have already configured AzureRM Subscription. Once it has completed successfully, we can select **App Service Name**. Click on the down arrow and the **Azure Web Apps** available in the configured **AzureRM subscription** will show in the list:

Go to **Select File Or Folder** and click on the three dots (**...**); go to the **PetClinic-Maven** and select the **WAR** file created after successful execution of build definition.

Our **Release Definitions** will pick this WAR file and deploy it in Azure Web Apps.

Click on **OK**.

Now, we are all set to execute the **Release Definitions**, but before that, we need to save the **Release Definitions**:

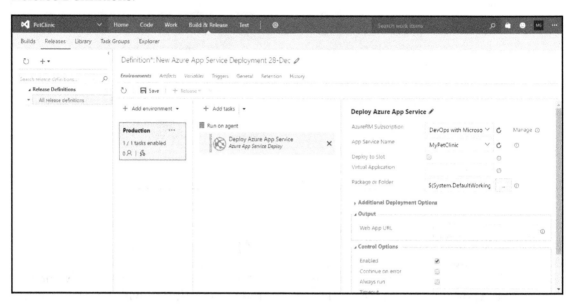

Click on the **Save** button and it will open a new dialog box. Provide a **Comment** and click on **OK** to save the release definition in VSTS:

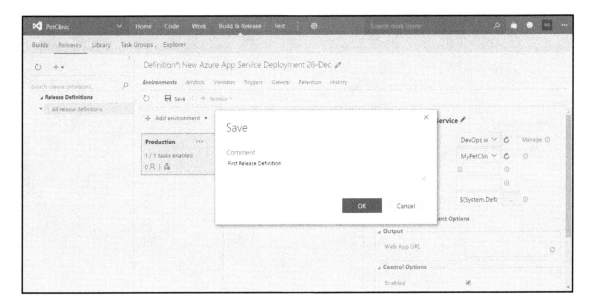

Verify that you have saved the release definition.

The **Triggers** section allows us to schedule when the new release should be created. We can set it when a new artifact version is available, or in other words, when a build definition execution has successfully completed:

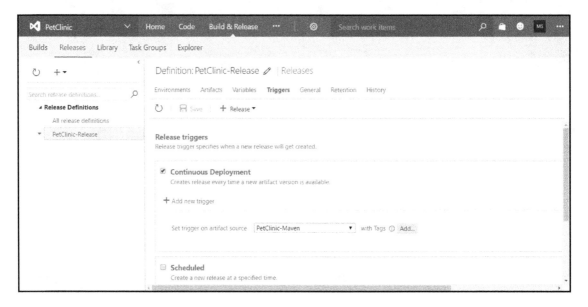

To check end-to-end automation, we will start build definition execution. So, once it is successful, it will trigger a release definition. Save the release definition and click on **Queue new build....**

Queue build for PetClinic-Maven build definition will trigger release definition if it is completed successfully. Click on **OK**:

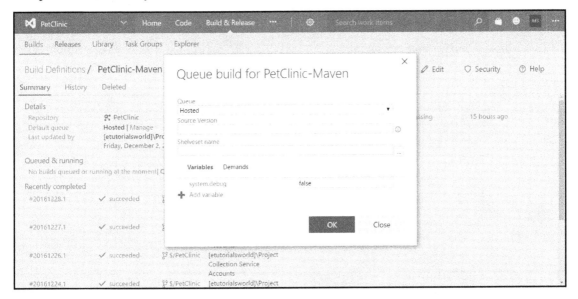

Once the build definition has successfully completed, the **PetClinic-Release** release definition will be triggered. Its job is to deploy the `.war` artifact into Azure App Services.

Deployment **Failed**! Let's find out why this deployment has failed.

Release definition execution has failed. Let's try to troubleshoot the issue:

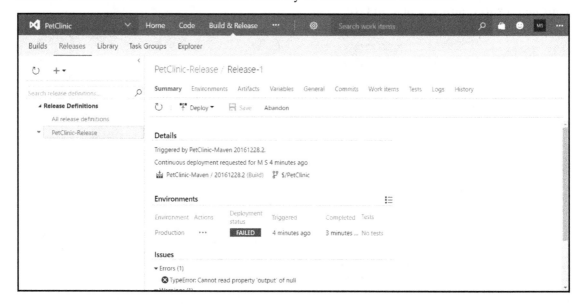

Verify the **History** first: we can see that release definition was triggered but deployment has failed:

Let's find out the likely cause of this failure from the logs.

Go to the **Logs** section and verify the release definition execution steps. It clearly indicates that it is the final deployment operation that has failed:

Click on the failed step, that is **Deploy Azure App Service**:

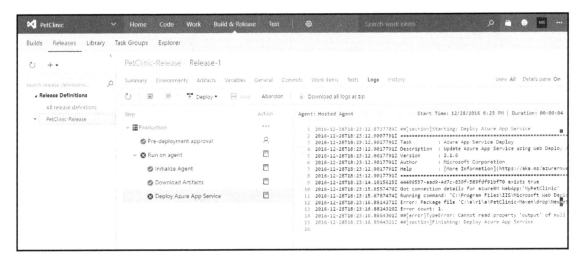

After closely examining the logs, we can see that it is mentioned that `.war` does not have a `.zip` file extension.

Remember, we selected `petclinic.war` and not `petclinic.zip`, so it is deploying the `.war` with this task; we need to have a `.zip` file and not a WAR file.

How to solve this?

If we can convert the WAR file into a **.zip** file, then it can be done and it should happen automatically:

The best way is to use any task that can convert `.war` in to a `.zip` file. So let's do it.

1. Click on **Add Task** and click on the **Marketplace** link:

It will open a new Marketplace window.

2. Find **Trackyon**:

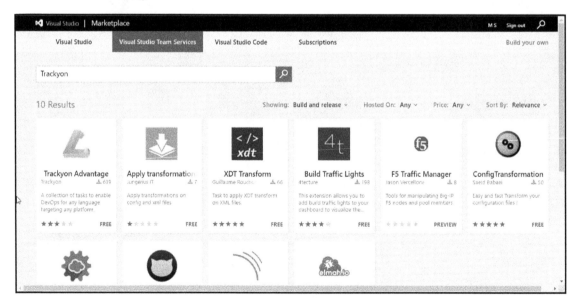

Before deployment, we will convert the WAR file into a ZIP file using **Trackyon**. Once that is done, our deployment on Azure Web Apps should work.

3. Click on **Install:**
4. Select the VSTS account where we want to install **Trackyon**.
5. Click on **Continue**:
6. Click on **Proceed to the account**.
7. Click on **Close:**

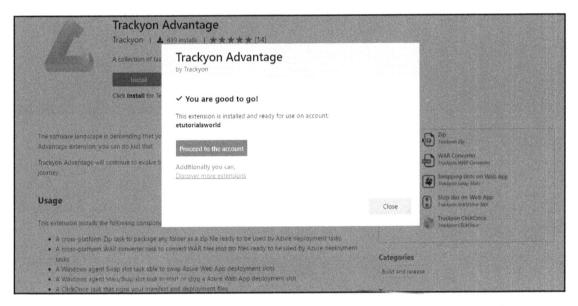

After installation, our next task is to add that task in the release definition so that, before deployment into Azure Web Apps, the WAR file is converted into a ZIP file.

8. Select the **Trackyon WAR converter** task.
9. Click on **Close:**

10. Select the folder where the WAR file is located:
11. Select the folder where the ZIP file should be created:
12. Now our release definition has two tasks to perform:

- Convert `.war` in to a `.zip` file.
- Deploy the `.zip` file into **Azure Web Apps**:

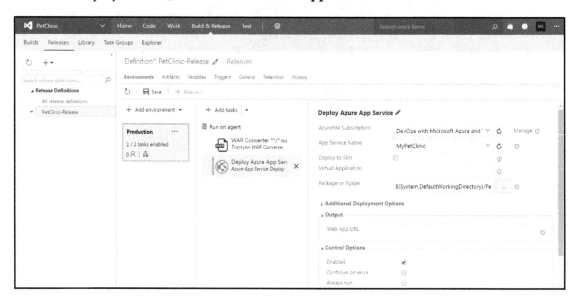

13. Go to the **PetClinic-Maven** build definition and click on **Queue new build...**
14. **Build** will start when the hosted agent is available.

Wait till build execution has completed successfully.

As we have configured our release definition for continuous delivery, the successful build definition execution will trigger our release definition to achieve end-to-end automation.

Note the **Build** number **Build 20161230.2**:

This build will trigger the release definition if completed successfully.

Summary

In this chapter, we have looked at different ways to deploy an application package into a local Tomcat server using Jenkins plugins, into a Docker container, into AWS Elastic Beanstalk, into Microsoft Azure App Services using FTP, and into Microsoft Azure App Services using Visual Studio Team Services.

If we observe the previous automation, it is one of the ways to deploy an application in a web server that is available locally or in the cloud using different ways, such as script, plugin, and VSTS.

Build definition was all about continuous integration, while release definition is all about continuous delivery. Hence, we have covered CI and CD till now, using different tools that are open source and commercial.

In the next chapter, we will cover automated testing (functional and load testing), so that we can consider it as a part of continuous testing.

We will use Selenium and Apache JMeter for functional testing and load testing respectively in a local and a cloud environment.

6
Automated Testing (Functional and Load Testing)

"Most people overestimate what they can do in one year and underestimate what they can do in ten years."

- Bill Gates

In this chapter, we will learn about the various types of testing that can be carried out after deploying an application in a non-prod environment. Continuous testing is extremely important to verify an application's functionality, performance, and so on. Automated testing will not only speed up the verification process, but it will also standardize the way testing is done in an effective manner. Our focus will be on simple functional testing to see how we can perform it, and load testing using the open source and commercial tools or services available.

We will create a sample functional test using Selenium and then execute it in Eclipse IDE for verification of its results. We will also integrate a Selenium-based Maven project with Jenkins so we can execute that functional test in Jenkins itself and make it a part of our end-to-end automation objective.

For load testing, we will create a sample load test using Apache JMeter GUI, and then use the saved `.jmx` file in Jenkins for load test execution from Jenkins.

This chapter will cover the following topics:

- Selenium-based functional testing for web applications using Eclipse
- Selenium and Jenkins integration
- Load testing with URL-based tests in **Visual Studio Team System** (**VSTS**)
- Load testing using Apache JMeter

Functional testing using Selenium

In this chapter, we will use Selenium and Eclipse for a functional test case execution. Let's go step by step to create a sample functional test case and then execute it using Jenkins.

The PetClinic project is a Maven-based spring application and we will create a test case using Eclipse and Maven. Hence, we will utilize the **m2eclipse** plugin in Eclipse.

We have installed Eclipse Java EE IDE for Web Developers, Version: Mars.2 Release (4.5.2), Build ID: 20160218-0600:

1. Go to the Eclipse marketplace and install the **Maven Integration** for Eclipse plugin.
2. Create a **Maven Project** using a wizard in Eclipse:

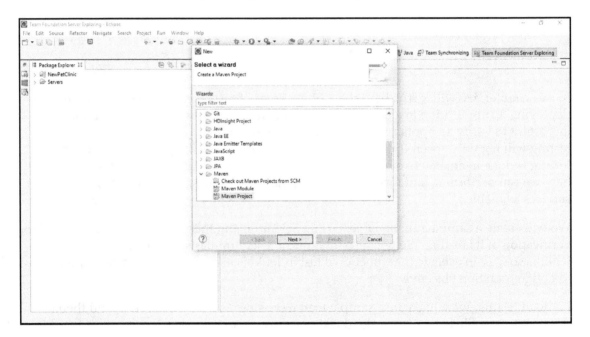

3. Select **Create a simple project (skip archetype selection)** and click on **Next**:

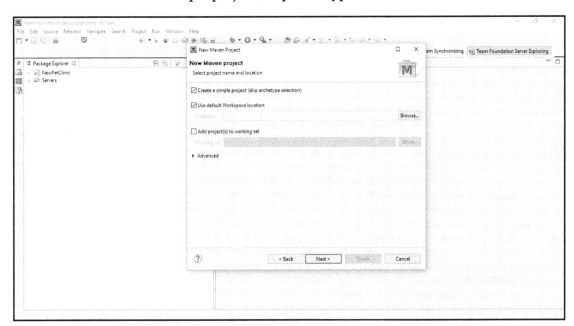

4. Go through the wizard and create a project. It will take some time to create a project in Eclipse. Provide **Artifact**, **Version**, **Packaging**, **Name**, and **Description**. Click on **Finish**.

5. Wait until the Maven project is created and configured. Make sure that Maven is installed and configured properly. In the case of Maven behind proxy, configure the proxy details into `conf.xml`, available in the `Maven` directory.

6. In `Pom.xml`, we need to add **Maven**, **Selenium**, **TestNG**, and **JUnit** dependencies in the `<project>` node. The following is a modified `Pom.xml`:

```
<project xmlns="http://maven.apache.org/POM/4.0.0"
xmlns:xsi="http://www.w3.org/2001/XMLSchema-instance"
  xsi:schemaLocation="http://maven.apache.org/POM/4.0.0
http://maven.apache.org/xsd/maven-4.0.0.xsd">
  <modelVersion>4.0.0</modelVersion>
  <groupId>com.tiny</groupId>
  <artifactId>test</artifactId>
  <version>0.0.1-SNAPSHOT</version>
  <name>test</name>
  <build>
    <plugins>
      <plugin>
        <groupId>org.apache.maven.plugins</groupId>
```

```
            <artifactId>maven-compiler-plugin</artifactId>
            <version>3.6.1</version>
            <configuration>
              <source>1.8</source>
              <target>1.8</target>
            </configuration>
          </plugin>
          <plugin>
            <groupId>org.apache.maven.plugins</groupId>
            <artifactId>maven-surefire-plugin</artifactId>
            <version>2.19.1</version>
            <configuration>
              <suiteXmlFiles>
                <suiteXmlFile>testng.xml</suiteXmlFile>
              </suiteXmlFiles>
            </configuration>
          </plugin>
        </plugins>
      </build>
      <dependencies>
        <dependency>
          <groupId>junit</groupId>
          <artifactId>junit</artifactId>
          <version>3.8.1</version>
          <scope>test</scope>
        </dependency>
        <dependency>
          <groupId>org.seleniumhq.selenium</groupId>
          <artifactId>selenium-java</artifactId>
          <version>3.0.1</version>
        </dependency>
        <dependency>
          <groupId>org.testng</groupId>
          <artifactId>testng</artifactId>
          <version>6.8</version>
          <scope>test</scope>
        </dependency>
      </dependencies>
    </project>
```

7. Save `pom.xml` after adding these changes and build the project again from the
   Project menu. It will download new dependencies:

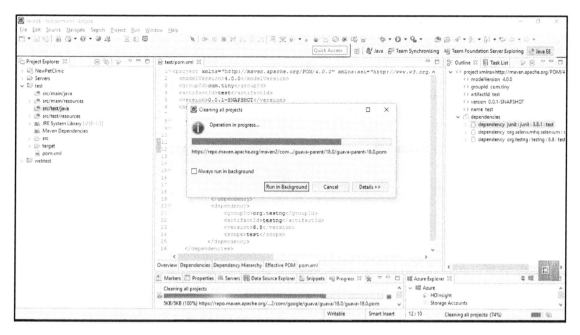

8. Click on the **Details** button of the dialog box to verify the operation in progress.

9. The next task is to write the TestNG class. Install the **TestNG** plugin. Go to **Help** and click on **Install New Software**. Add **Repository**:

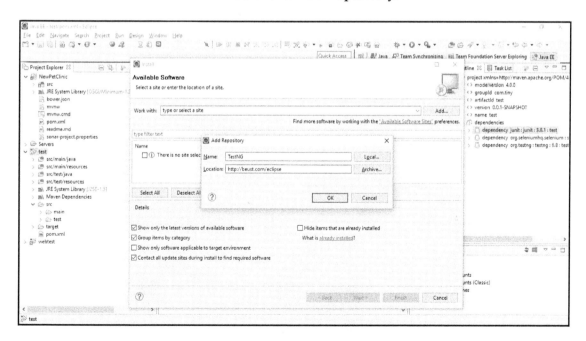

10. Select the items we need to install:

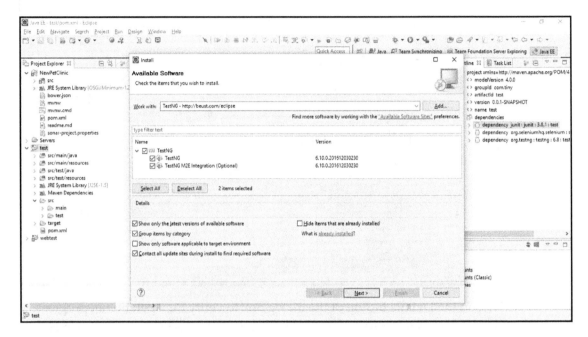

11. Review all the items that need to be installed and click on **Next**.

12. Accept the license and click on **Finish**.

13. Verify the installation progress in Eclipse.

14. Now let's create a `TestNG` class:

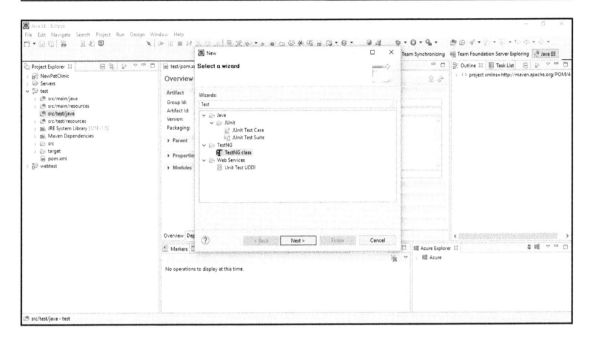

15. Provide a **Class name**:

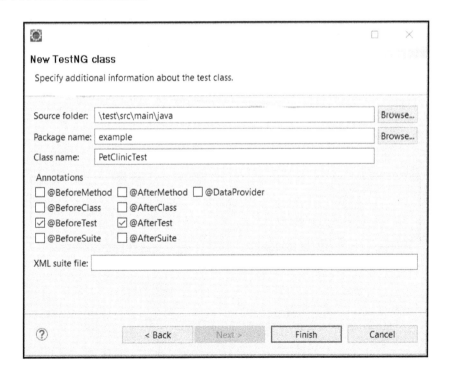

16. Give a **Package name** and click on **Finish**.

17. The newly created class will look like the following screenshot:

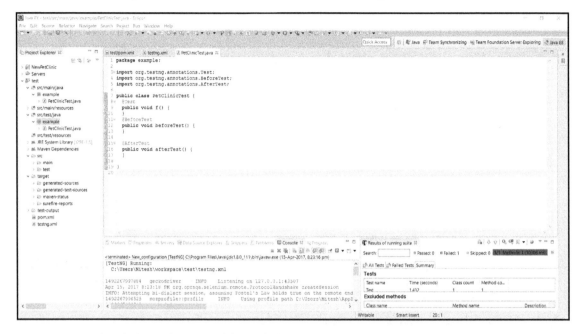

18. Right-click on the `test` file and click on **TestNG, convert to TestNG**.

19. It will create a `testing.xml` file that has details about the test suite:

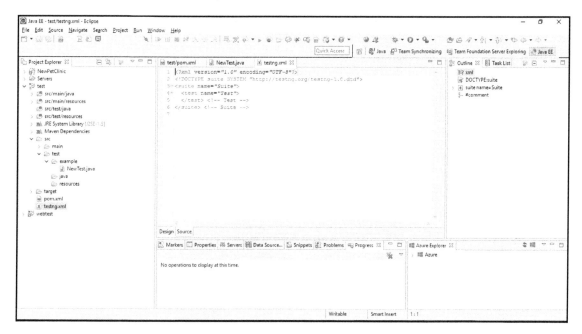

20. Right-click on **Project** and click on **Run Configurations**.

21. Right-click on **TestNG** and click on **New**:

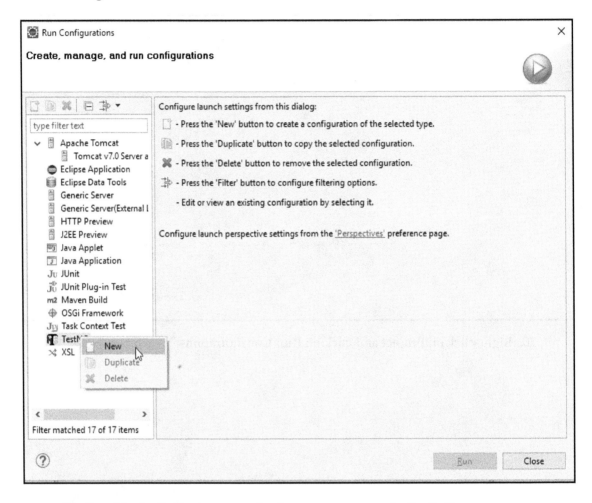

22. Provide the **Project** name and select `testing.xml` in the **Suite**.
23. Click **OK** and **Apply**.
24. Click on **Run**:

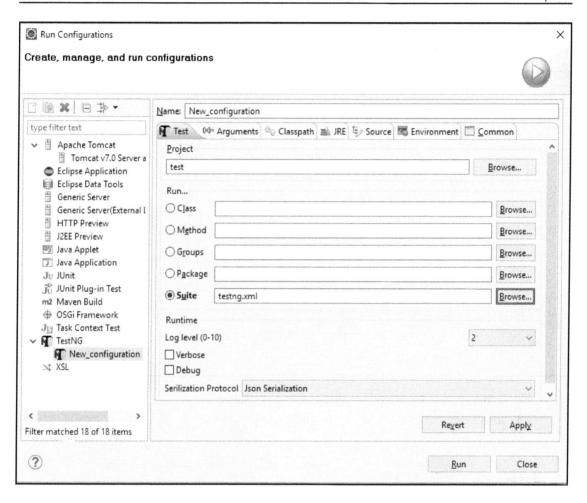

25. If Windows Firewall blocks it then click on **Allow Access**.

26. There is no configuration available in `testing.xml` for execution, hence, even if Maven execution runs successfully, no suite will be executed:

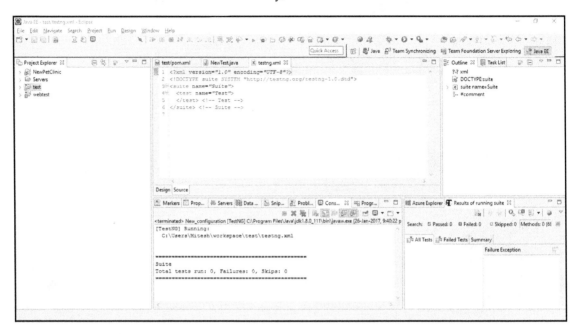

27. Generate the `TestNG` class under the `test` folder.

28. Select `location`, `suite name`, and `class name`:

```
<?xml version="1.0" encoding="UTF-8"?>
<!DOCTYPE suite SYSTEM "http://testng.org/testng-1.0.dtd">
<suite name="Suite">
<test name="Test">
<classes>
<class name="example.PetClinicTest"/>
</classes>
</test><!-- Test -->
</suite><!-- Suite -->
```

29. Go to `https://github.com/mozilla/geckodriver/releases` and download a version.

30. Extract the file available in the downloaded ZIP file based on the system configuration we have. In our case, we have downloaded `geckodriver-v0.13.0-win64`.

31. Click on it and verify the driver details.

Let's write some code as well. It will check whether the title of the web page contains a specific string or not. The result or the outcome of the following code is based on the title of the page. If it contains a given string then the test case will pass; else it will fail:

```java
package example;

importjava.io.File;
importorg.openqa.selenium.WebDriver;
importorg.openqa.selenium.firefox.FirefoxDriver;
importorg.testng.Assert;
importorg.testng.annotations.Test;
importorg.testng.annotations.BeforeTest;
importorg.testng.annotations.AfterTest;
public class PetClinicTest {
  private WebDriver driver;
    @Test
    public void testPetClinic() {
      driver.get("http://localhost:8090/petclinic/");
      String title = driver.getTitle();
      Assert.assertTrue(title.contains("a Spring Frameworkk"));
    }
    @BeforeTest
    public void beforeTest() {
      File file = new File("F:\\##DevOpsBootCamp\\geckodriver-v0.13.0-
win64\\geckodriver.exe");
      System.setProperty("webdriver.gecko.driver", file.getAbsolutePath());
      driver = new FirefoxDriver();
    }
    @AfterTest
    public void afterTest() {
      driver.quit();
    }
}
```

The same file is available in IDE, shown as follows.

Let's run the Maven test again from Eclipse.

The following is the output when the test case is executed successfully:

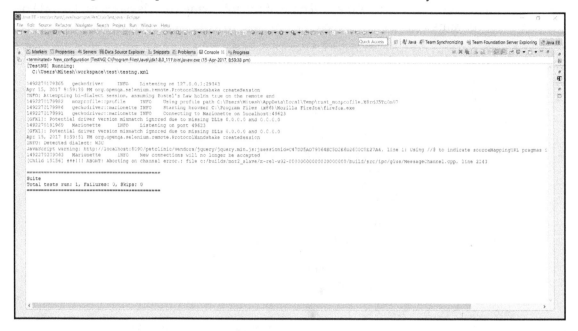

1. Verify the **All Tests** tab in the **Results of running suite** section in Eclipse. We can see successful execution here:

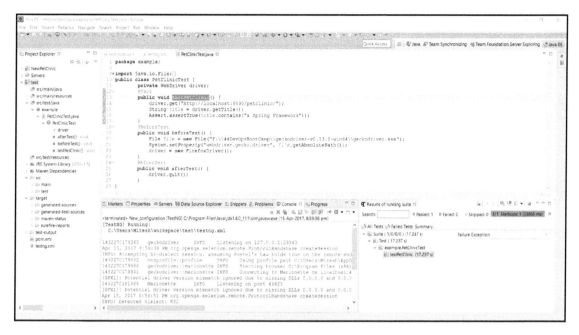

2. Verify the **Failed Tests** tab in the **Results of running suite** section in Eclipse.

3. Verify the **Summary** tab in the **Results of running suite** section in Eclipse in the successful scenario.

4. In the code, change the text available for title comparison so the test case fails.

5. Verify the output in **Console**:

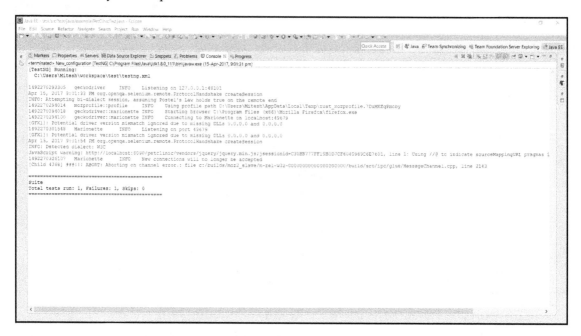

6. Verify the **All Tests** tab in the **Results of running suite** section in Eclipse and notice the failure icon:

7. Verify the **Failed Tests** tab in the **Results of running suite** section in Eclipse.
8. Click on **testPetClinic** and verify the **Failure Exception**.
9. Verify the **Summary** tab in the **Results of running suite** section in Eclipse.

So, we have created a sample test case based on Selenium to verify the title of the PetClinic home page.

Functional test execution in Jenkins

Now let's try to execute the same from Jenkins:

1. Check in the **Test Project** in **Repository**. Create a `PetClinic-FuncTest` freestyle job in Jenkins.
2. In the **Build** section, provide **Root POM** location and **Goals and options** to execute:

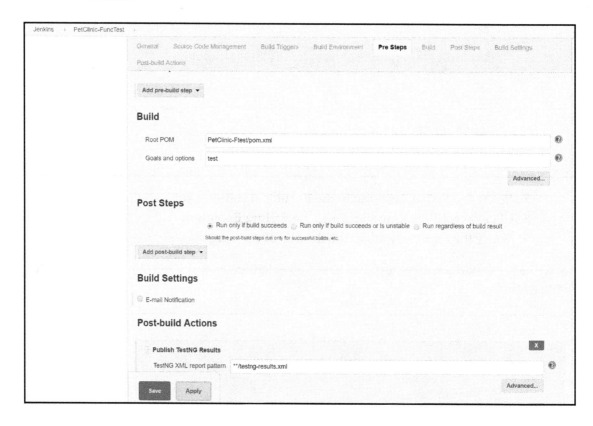

3. **Save** the build job and click on **Build now**.
4. Verify the execution of the build job in the **Console** output.
5. It will open a Mozilla Firefox window and open a URL that is given in the code. This requires our PetClinic application to be deployed in a web server and running without any issues:

```
Jan 28, 2017 11:24:13 PM org.openqa.selenium.os.UnixProcess destroy
SEVERE: Unable to kill process with PID 9432
Tests run: 1, Failures: 0, Errors: 0, Skipped: 0, Time elapsed: 20.204 sec - in TestSuite

Results :

Tests run: 1, Failures: 0, Errors: 0, Skipped: 0

[JENKINS] Recording test results
[INFO] ------------------------------------------------------------------
[INFO] BUILD SUCCESS
[INFO] ------------------------------------------------------------------
[INFO] Total time: 35.953 s
[INFO] Finished at: 2017-01-28T23:24:18+05:30
[INFO] Final Memory: 16M/167M
[INFO] ------------------------------------------------------------------
Waiting for Jenkins to finish collecting data
[JENKINS] Archiving C:\Users\Mitesh\.jenkins\workspace\PetClinic-FuncTest\PetClinic-Ftest\pom.xml to com.tiny/test/0.0.1-SNAPSHOT/test-
0.0.1-SNAPSHOT.pom
channel stopped
TestNG Reports Processing: START
Looking for TestNG results report in workspace using pattern: **/testng-results.xml
testng-results.xml was last modified before this build started. Ignoring it.
Saving reports...
Processing 'C:\Users\Mitesh\.jenkins\jobs\PetClinic-FuncTest\builds\6\testng\testng-results.xml'
TestNG Reports Processing: FINISH
Warning: you have no plugins providing access control for builds, so falling back to legacy behavior of permitting any downstream builds
to be triggered
Triggering a new build of PetClinic-LoadTest
Finished: SUCCESS
```

Page generated: Apr 17, 2017 5:42.23 PM IST   REST API   Jenkins ver. 2.32.1

6. Now make a change in the code so title verification fails and execute the build job.

7. There is a failure marked in the **Console** output in Jenkins:

```
-------------------------------------------------
  T E S T S
-------------------------------------------------
Running TestSuite
Tests run: 3, Failures: 1, Errors: 0, Skipped: 2, Time elapsed: 1.135 sec <<< FAILURE! - in TestSuite
beforeTest(example.NewTest)  Time elapsed: 0.685 sec  <<< FAILURE!
java.lang.IllegalStateException: The driver executable does not exist: C:\Users\Mitesh\Downloads\geckodriver-v0.13.0-win64\geckodriver.exe
        at example.NewTest.beforeTest(NewTest.java:33)


Results :

Failed tests:
  NewTest.beforeTest:33 » IllegalState The driver executable does not exist: C:\...

Tests run: 3, Failures: 1, Errors: 0, Skipped: 2

[ERROR] There are test failures.

Please refer to C:\Users\Mitesh\.jenkins\workspace\PetClinic-FuncTest\PetClinic-Ftest\target\surefire-reports for the individual test
results.
[JENKINS] Recording test results
[INFO] ------------------------------------------------------------------------
[INFO] BUILD SUCCESS
[INFO] ------------------------------------------------------------------------
[INFO] Total time: 20.679 s
[INFO] Finished at: 2017-02-27T21:52:38+05:30
[INFO] Final Memory: 14M/68M
[INFO] ------------------------------------------------------------------------
[JENKINS] Archiving C:\Users\Mitesh\.jenkins\workspace\PetClinic-FuncTest\PetClinic-Ftest\pom.xml to com.tiny/test/0.0.1-SNAPSHOT/test-
0.0.1-SNAPSHOT.pom
channel stopped
TestNG Reports Processing: START
Looking for TestNG results report in workspace using pattern: **/testng-results.xml
testng-results.xml was last modified before this build started. Ignoring it.
Saving reports...
Processing 'C:\Users\Mitesh\.jenkins\jobs\PetClinic-FuncTest\builds\7\testng\testng-results.xml'
TestNG Reports Processing: FINISH
Warning: you have no plugins providing access control for builds, so falling back to legacy behavior of permitting any downstream builds
to be triggered
Finished: UNSTABLE
```

8. Go to the **Project** dashboard and verify the graphs for **TestNG Results**:

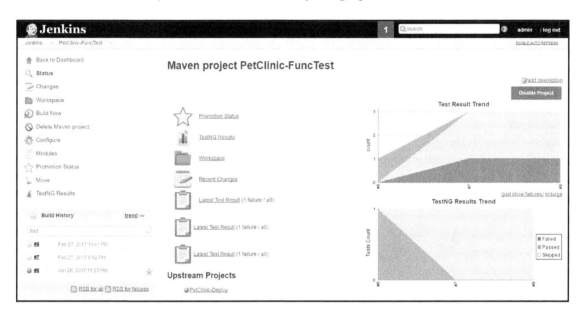

We have seen how to execute Selenium-based test cases in Jenkins.

In the next section, we will see how to execute a load test using Jenkins.

Load test execution using Jenkins

The steps are as follows:

1. Open the Apache Jmeter console. Create a **Test Plan**.
2. Right-click on the **Test Plan** and click on **Add**; select **Threads (Users)**.
3. Select **Thread Group**.
4. Provide **Thread Group** name.
5. In **Thread Group** properties, provide **Number of Threads**, **Ramp-up Period**, and **Loop Count**.

6. Right-click on **Thread Group**. Click on **Add**. Click on **Sampler**. Click on **HTTP Request**.

7. In **HTTP Request**, provide **Server Name or IP**. In our case, it will be localhost or an IP address.

8. Give the **Port Number** where your web server is running.

9. Select the **Get** method and provide a path to the load test:

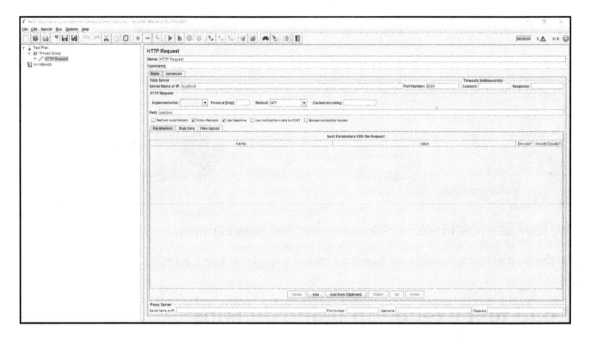

10. Save the `.jmx` file.

11. Now let's create a Jenkins job.

12. Create a freestyle job in Jenkins:

13. Add the **Build** step **Execute Windows batch command**.
    1. Add the following command. Replace the location of `jmeter.bat` based on the installation directory and the location of the `.jmx` file too:

```
C:\apache-jmeter-3.0\bin\jmeter.bat -
Jjmeter.save.saveservice.output_format=xml -n -t
C:\Users\Mitesh\Desktop\PetClinic.jmx -l Test.jtl
```

14. Add a **Post-build Actions. Publish Performance test result report** add **/*.jtl file.

15. Click on **Build now**:

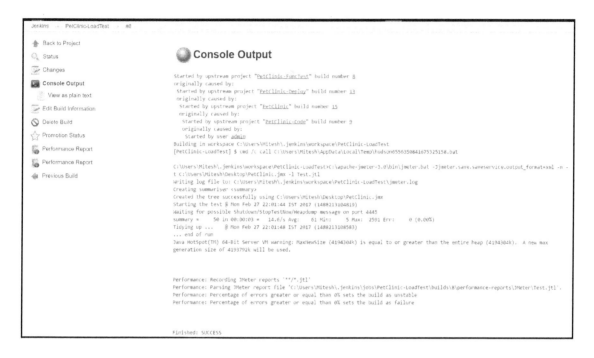

16. Verify **Performance Trend** on the **Project** dashboard.
17. Click on **Performance Trend**:

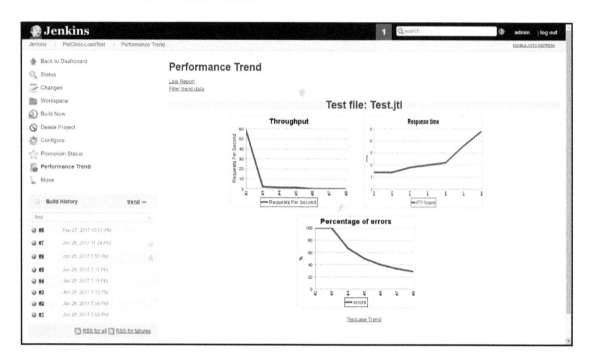

18. Verify **Performance Breakdown**.

In the next section, we will see how to perform load testing of a web application deployed in Microsoft Azure App Services using the options available in VSTS.

Load testing using a URL-based test and Apache JMeter for Microsoft Azure

Once we have deployed our application in Azure App Services successfully, we can perform load testing on the Azure App Service or Azure Web Apps. Let's see how we can use Visual Studio Team Services to perform testing.

URL-based test

1. In the top menu bar, click on **Load test**. Let's create our first test in the VSTS and execute it.

2. Click on **New** and select **URL based test**:

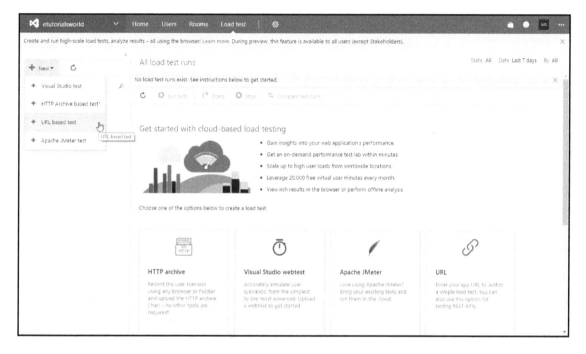

3. Verify the **HTTP method** and **URL**:

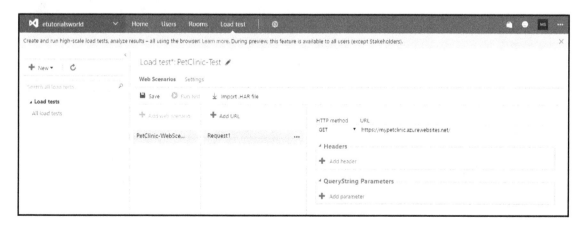

4. Click on **Settings**; provide input in the different parameters based on need:

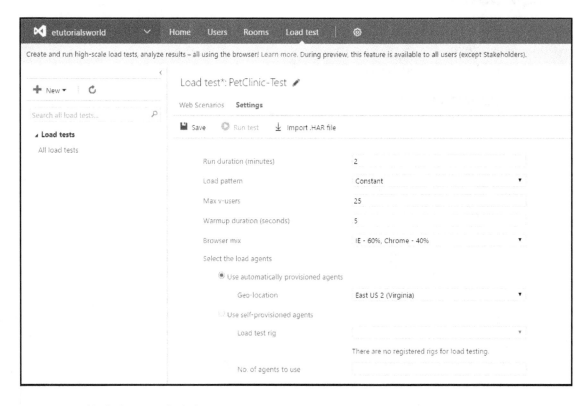

5. Click **Save** and click on **Run test**.
6. Load testing is in progress:

7. Verify the complete test data as and when it is available in the VSTS portal.
8. Verify the final summary of the URL-based test execution in VSTS:

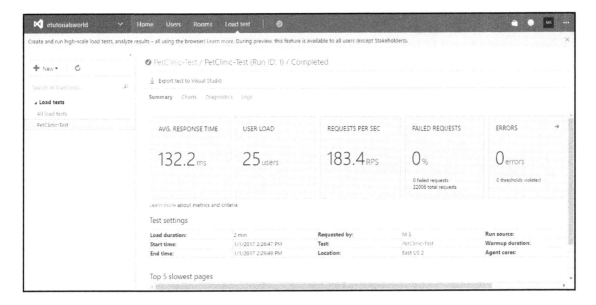

9. We will also get **Performance** and **Throughput** charts after the test execution in VSTS:

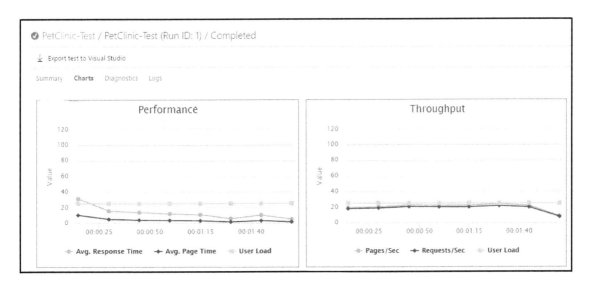

10. Verify tests and error-related details too.

We have seen how a URL-based test can be performed on an Azure Web App. In the next section, we will cover how to use Apache JMeter for load testing.

Apache JMeter

We often need to verify how much load an application serves so, based on it, we can check many functions or bottlenecks to improve the performance so it can serve as many requests as it can with efficiency. In this section, we'll look into how to execute Apache JMeter testing. We will execute a load test on the PetClinic application deployed on Azure App Services.

For more details on this topic, go to
`http://jmeter.apache.org/usermanual/`.

To begin the execution, follow these steps:

1. Download Apache JMeter from `http://jmeter.apache.org/`.
2. Start it and create a **Thread Group** in Apache JMeter. Here, we mention **Number of Threads (users)**, **Ramp Up Period (in seconds)**, and **Loop Count**:

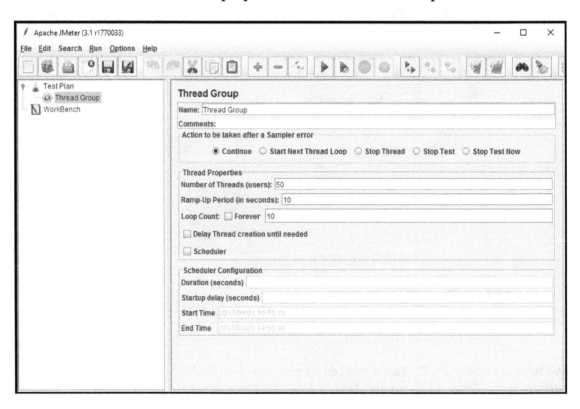

3. Right-click on the **Thread Group** and click on **Add**.
4. Select **Sampler** and click on **HTTP Request**:

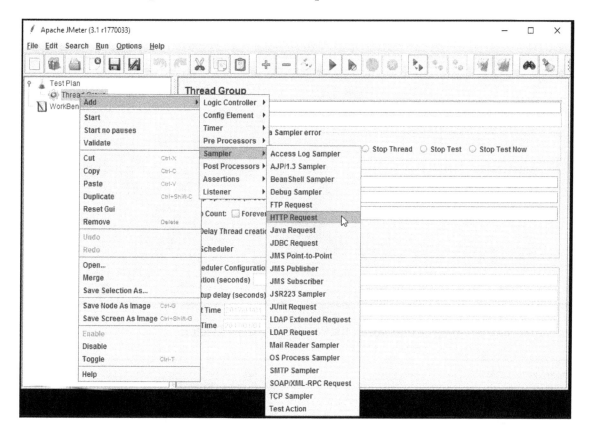

5. Provide the Azure Web App URL in the server name and select HTTPS protocol:

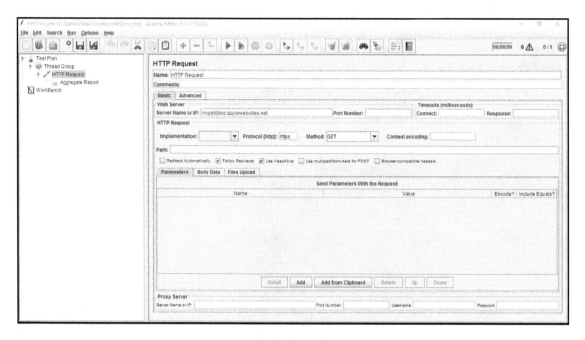

6. Execute the test and verify the result in Apache JMeter:

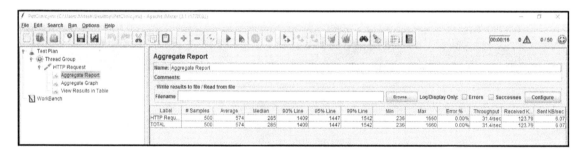

7. Add **Aggregate Graph** in **HTTP Request**:

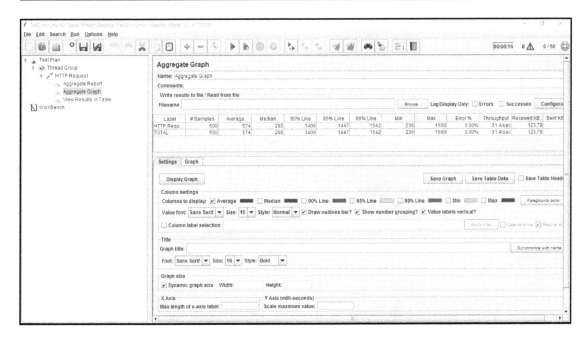

8. After the load test execution, verify the graph.
9. For more details, click on **View Results in Table**:

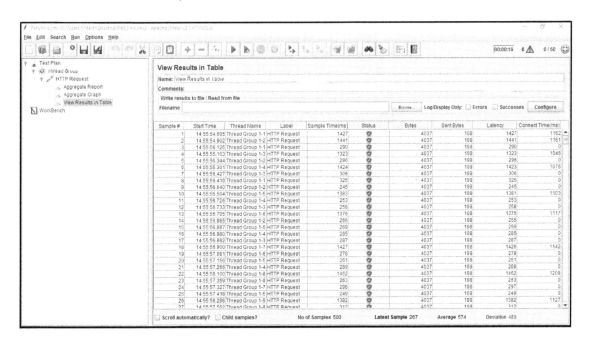

We can execute an Apache JMeter test in the VSTS too.

Progress toward execution as follows:

1. Click on **New** and select **Apache JMeter test**:

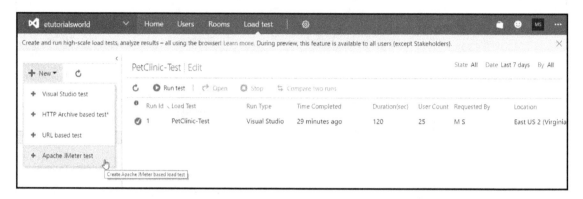

2. We will use the same JMX file that we used earlier to load test an Azure Web App.

3. Select **Load duration** and **Load location** as well. Click on **Run Test**:

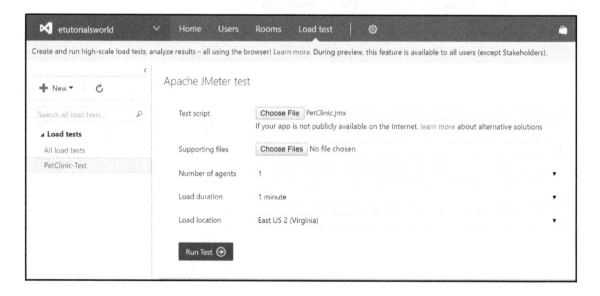

Summary

"Testing is a skill. While this may come as a surprise to some people it is a simple fact."

- Fewster and Graham

It is extremely important to verify the quality of an application. Testing is that part of application life cycle management that we can't ignore. It is one of the pillars of a quality product.

Hence, it is extremely important to make testing a habit. Different types of testing keep an eye on different dimensions of quality, and that makes an application robust.

Continuous testing plays a significant part as we talk about continuous integration and continuous delivery. If that part is automated, continuous testing in automated mode helps to achieve robustness faster and to keep pace with a shorter time to market.

In this chapter, we have covered functional and load testing integrated with Jenkins.

In the next chapter, we will see how all the operations we have performed till now can be orchestrated in sequence. That will give us the feel of end-to-end automation. It is more about creating a pipeline in Jenkins and configuring triggers in build and release definition so that application life cycle management steps can be automated.

7
Orchestration - End-to-End Automation

"The key to following the continuous delivery path is to continually question your own assumptions about what's possible."

- Jeff Sussna

In this chapter, we will discuss different ways to automate application life cycle management, using orchestration available via open source and commercial alternatives.

We will be using Jenkins plugins and Visual Studio Team Services tasks to orchestrate and automate all the activities that are performed during application life cycle management.

We will cover the following topics in this chapter:

- End-to-end automation orchestration of application life cycle management using Jenkins
- End-to-end automation using Jenkins, Chef, and AWS EC2
- End-to-end automation using Jenkins and AWS Elastic Beanstalk
- End-to-end automation using Jenkins and Microsoft Azure app services
- End-to-end automation orchestration of application life cycle management using VSTS

End-to-end automation of application life cycle management using Jenkins

In Chapter 2, *Continous Integration*, we created a build job that performs the following tasks:

1. Static code analysis of the PetClinic web application:

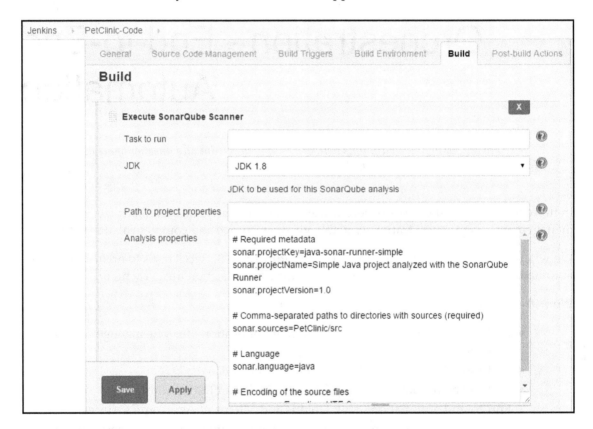

2. Successful execution of static code analysis will show a URL pointing to the SonaQube dashboard for a specific project in Jenkins dashboard.

3. Verification of the Jenkins dashboard with all the analysis details:

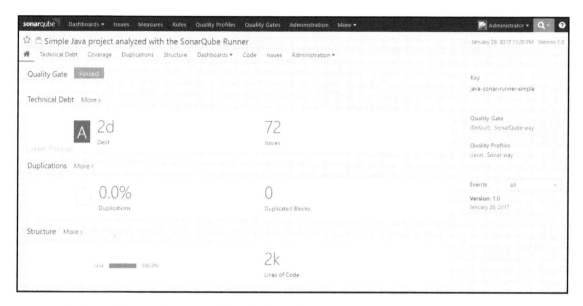

4. Compilation of source files and unit test execution:

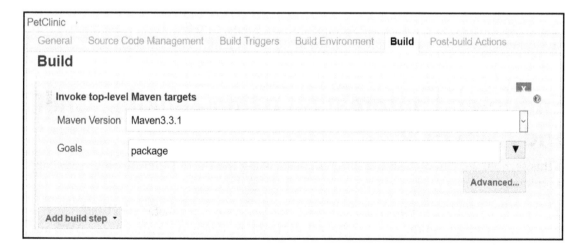

5. Unit test results will be available in the Jenkins project dashboard itself.

6. Creation of package files:

```
Jenkins  ›  PetClinic  ›  #1
          [INFO]
          [INFO] --- maven-war-plugin:2.3:war (default-war) @ spring-petclinic ---
          [INFO] Packaging webapp
          [INFO] Assembling webapp [spring-petclinic] in [/home/mitesh/.jenkins/workspace
          /PetClinic/target/spring-petclinic-4.2.5-SNAPSHOT]
          [INFO] Processing war project
          [INFO] Copying webapp resources [/home/mitesh/.jenkins/workspace/PetClinic
          /src/main/webapp]
          [INFO] Webapp assembled in [12697 msecs]
          [INFO] Building war: /home/mitesh/.jenkins/workspace/PetClinic/target
          /petclinic.war
          [INFO] ------------------------------------------------------------------------
          [INFO] BUILD SUCCESS
          [INFO] ------------------------------------------------------------------------
          [INFO] Total time: 03:14 min
          [INFO] Finished at: 2016-04-27T12:15:29-07:00
          [INFO] Final Memory: 27M/214M
          [INFO] ------------------------------------------------------------------------
          Finished: SUCCESS
```

Once our package file is ready we can deploy it in the AWSEC2 instance, Microsoft Azure Virtual Machine, AWS Elastic Beanstalk, Microsoft Azure App Services, containers, or any physical machine that is accessible from the system that Jenkins is installed on.

End-to-end automation using Jenkins, Chef, and AWS EC2

In this section, we will orchestrate different tasks using the **Build Pipeline** plugin available in Jenkins.

In Chapter 4, *Cloud Computing and Configuration Management*, we installed a Chef workstation, configured the hosted Chef account, and installed knife plugins for AWS and Microsoft Azure.

We created an instance in AWS EC2 using the following command:

```
[root@devops1 Desktop]# knife ec2 server create -I ami-1ecae776 -f t2.micro
-N DevOpsVMonAWS --aws-access-key-id '< Your Access Key ID >' --aws-secret-
access-key '< Your Secret Access Key >' -S book --identity-file book.pem --
ssh-user ec2-user -r role[v-tomcat]
```

We created a virtual machine in Microsoft Azure using the following command:

```
[root@devops1 Desktop]# knife azure server create --azure-dns-name
'distechnodemo' --azure-vm-name 'dtserver02' --azure-vm-size 'Small' -N
DevOpsVMonAzure2 --azure-storage-account 'classicstorage9883' --bootstrap-
protocol 'cloud-api' --azure-source-image
'5112500ae3b842c8b9c604889f8753c3__OpenLogic-CentOS-67-20160310' --azure-
service-location 'Central US' --ssh-user 'dtechno' --ssh-password
'cloud@321' -r role[v-tomcat] --ssh-port 22
```

We verified the AWS EC2 instance and Microsoft Azure Virtual Machine registration in the hosted Chef.

We executed both the commands from the command prompt. In Jenkins, we can execute commands for Windows, Linux, or Mac. We can execute the same commands from a Jenkins build job by creating a freestyle job.

Configuring SSH authentication using a key

A Chef workstation installed on a virtual machine is accessible from a system where we have installed Jenkins. We can create a virtual machine using a virtual box or a VMware workstation on a laptop; and can also then install CentOS 6 or 7 and configure the Chef workstation the way we did in Chapter 4, *Cloud Computing and Configuration Management*.

Before starting with the configuration of end-to-end automation and orchestration using a build pipeline plugin and upstream/downstream jobs, we will configure SSH authentication using a key.

The main objective behind configuring SSH authentication is to allow the Jenkins virtual machine to connect to the Chef workstation virtual machine. By doing this we can execute commands from the Jenkins machine on the Chef workstation. This way we can create an instance in AWS or the Azure cloud using the Chef workstation, and install a runtime environment on it to deploy the PetClinic application:

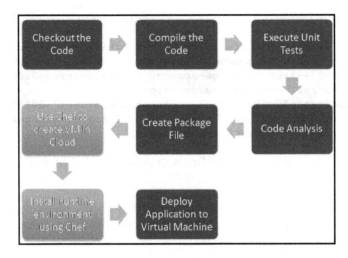

If we try to access the Chef workstation from Jenkins, it won't work, as we still need to configure a password-free configuration, because in the Jenkins job execution we can't wait in the middle of a flow to give a password. Let's configure password-free access on Jenkins to access the Chef workstation:

1. Open a terminal in a virtual machine where Jenkins is installed. Use `ssh-keygen` to create a new key:

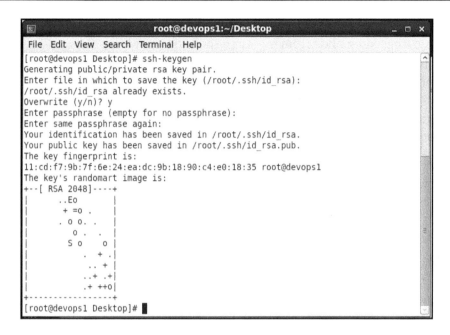

2. Verify the key on the local filesystem.
3. Copy the key to the remote host where the Chef workstation is configured using `ssh-copy-id`:

```
File  Edit  View  Search  Terminal  Help
[root@devops1 Desktop]# ssh-copy-id -i ~/.ssh/id_rsa.pub 192.168.0.106
Agent admitted failure to sign using the key.
root@192.168.0.106's password:
Now try logging into the machine, with "ssh '192.168.0.106'", and check in:

  .ssh/authorized_keys

to make sure we haven't added extra keys that you weren't expecting.

[root@devops1 Desktop]# ssh-copy-id -i ~/.ssh/id_rsa.pub mitesh@192.168.0.106
mitesh@192.168.0.106's password:
Now try logging into the machine, with "ssh 'mitesh@192.168.0.106'", and check i
n:

  .ssh/authorized_keys

to make sure we haven't added extra keys that you weren't expecting.
```

4. Now try to access the Chef workstation VM using the Jenkins build job by executing commands from `execute` shell commands.

5. If it fails, then try to access the Chef workstation from the Jenkins VM using the Terminal. If you get the **Agent admitted failure to sign using key** message, then execute the `ssh-add` command to fix the issue.

6. Once the connection is successful in the Terminal, execute the `ifconfig` command to find the IP address so that we find out on which virtual machine that command is executed:

```
[mitesh@devops1 Desktop]$ ssh-copy-id -i ~/.ssh/id_rsa.pub root@192.168.0.103
root@192.168.0.103's password:
Now try logging into the machine, with "ssh 'root@192.168.0.103'", and check in:

  .ssh/authorized_keys

to make sure we haven't added extra keys that you weren't expecting.

[mitesh@devops1 Desktop]$ ssh -t root@192.168.0.103
Agent admitted failure to sign using the key.
root@192.168.0.103's password:

[mitesh@devops1 Desktop]$ ssh-add
Identity added: /home/mitesh/.ssh/id_rsa (/home/mitesh/.ssh/id_rsa)
[mitesh@devops1 Desktop]$ ssh -t root@192.168.0.103
Last login: Thu Jul 28 12:21:56 2016 from 192.168.0.106
[root@devops1 ~]# ifconfig
eth5      Link encap:Ethernet  HWaddr 00:0C:29:91:3F:2F
          inet addr:192.168.0.103  Bcast:192.168.0.255  Mask:255.255.255.0
          inet6 addr: fe80::20c:29ff:fe91:3f2f/64 Scope:Link
          UP BROADCAST RUNNING MULTICAST  MTU:1500  Metric:1
          RX packets:2664 errors:0 dropped:0 overruns:0 frame:0
          TX packets:1727 errors:0 dropped:0 overruns:0 carrier:0
          collisions:0 txqueuelen:1000
          RX bytes:716002 (699.2 KiB)  TX bytes:197090 (192.4 KiB)

lo        Link encap:Local Loopback
          inet addr:127.0.0.1  Mask:255.0.0.0
          inet6 addr: ::1/128 Scope:Host
          UP LOOPBACK RUNNING  MTU:65536  Metric:1
          RX packets:50663 errors:0 dropped:0 overruns:0 frame:0
          TX packets:50663 errors:0 dropped:0 overruns:0 carrier:0
          collisions:0 txqueuelen:0
```

7. At this stage, our SSH connection is successful using a key that we created and configured instead of a password.

8. Now we have access to the Chef workstation from Jenkins' VM so we can execute knife commands from Jenkins on the Chef workstation. Our next goal is to try to create an instance in AWS using the Jenkins build job and the Chef workstation.

9. In a Jenkins build job, add a **Build** step, select **Execute shell**, and add the command shown here. We have already discussed `knife ec2` commands:

```
ssh -t -t root@192.168.1.36 "ifconfig; rvm use
2.1.0; knife ec2 server create -I ami-1ecae776 -f
t2.micro -N DevOpsVMonAWS1 --aws-access-key-id
'<YOUR ACCESS KEY ID>' --aws-secret-access-key
'<YOUR SECRET ACCESS KEY>' -S book --identity-file
book.pem --ssh-user ec2-user -r role[v-tomcat]"
```

10. Replace the Access Key ID and Secret Access Key with your own. Click on **Save**. Click on the **Build now** link to execute the build job.

11. Go to **Console Output** to check the progress:

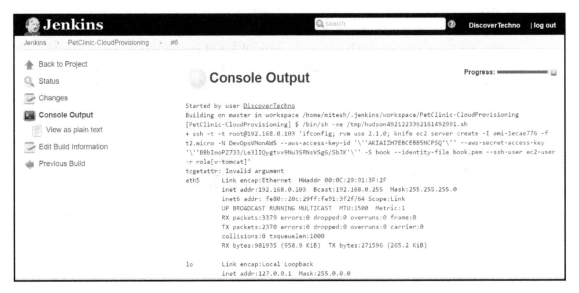

12. Inspect the logs; AWS instance creation has started.
13. Verify it in the AWS management console:

14. Before execution can go further, check whether the AWS security group has an entry for SSH access:

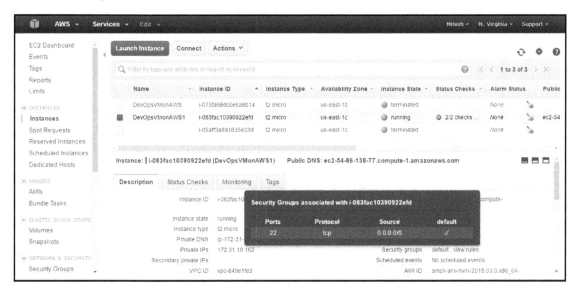

15. Once SSH access is available, it will start the Chef client installations.
16. In our case, it will start downloading the Chef client and installing it on the AWS instance that we have created using the Chef workstation:
17. Verify the Chef installation process on the console. Once the Chef client is installed on the AWS instance, it will start its first Chef client execution.
18. Observe the run list and synchronizing cookbooks. It will converge and start installing packages.
19. Verify the package installations.
20. It will also display `conf.xml`, where port-related details can be verified based on the configuration.

21. Once the package installation is finished, it will start service management.
22. Now, the Chef client execution has finished, and it will display related information for the AWS instance we created:

```
[36mec2-52-23-215-193.compute-1.amazonaws.com[0m

[36mec2-52-23-215-193.compute-1.amazonaws.com[0m Chef Client finished, 13/15 resources
seconds


[36mInstance ID[0m: i-024d3bf83022b89e4
[36mFlavor[0m: t2.micro
[36mImage[0m: ami-1ecae776
[36mRegion[0m: us-east-1
[36mAvailability Zone[0m: us-east-1d
[36mSecurity Groups[0m: default
[36mSecurity Group Ids[0m: default
[36mTags[0m: Name: DevOpsVMonAWS
[36mSSH Key[0m: book
[36mRoot Device Type[0m: ebs
[36mRoot Volume ID[0m: vol-00aae3951d7ed88bb
[36mRoot Device Name[0m: /dev/xvda
[36mRoot Device Delete on Terminate[0m: true


[35mBlock devices[0m
[35m===========================[0m
[36mDevice Name[0m: /dev/xvda
[36mVolume ID[0m: vol-00aae3951d7ed88bb
[36mDelete on Terminate[0m: true


[35m===========================[0m
[36mPublic DNS Name[0m: ec2-52-23-215-193.compute-1.amazonaws.com
[36mPublic IP Address[0m: 52.23.215.193
[36mPrivate DNS Name[0m: ip-172-31-31-133.ec2.internal
[36mPrivate IP Address[0m: 172.31.31.133
[36mEnvironment[0m: _default
[36mRun List[0m: role[v-tomcat]
Connection to 192.168.0.103 closed.
Finished: SUCCESS
```

23. Check the AWS management console for the successful status.
24. Verify the hosted Chef for the registered nodes:

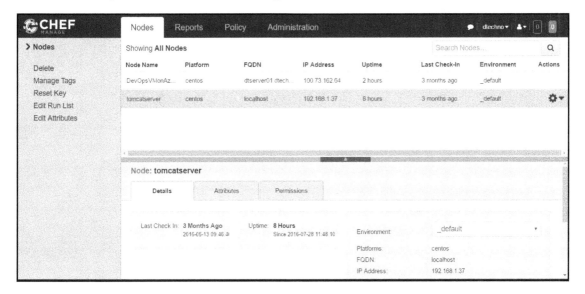

At this stage, we have an AWS instance ready that has Tomcat and Java installed so we can deploy our application easily. Now, we have all the resources ready to configure the build pipeline:

1. Go to **PetClinic-Code** job and select **Build other projects** from add **Post-build Actions**.

2. Enter **PetClinic** in **Projects to build**:

3. Here **PetClinic-Code** becomes an upstream project for PetClinic and PetClinic becomes a downstream project for **PetClinic-Code**. The **Build Pipeline** plugin needs relations established, using upstream and downstream projects for visualization.

4. Go to the **PetClinic-Code** job and select **Build other projects** from **Add Post-build Actions**.

5. Enter **PetClinic-CloudProvisioning** in **Projects to build**:

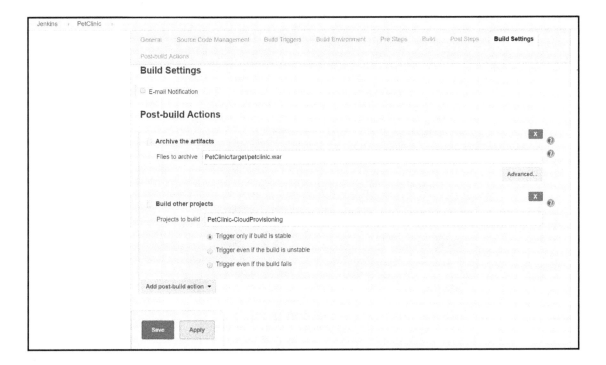

6. If this build job has executed successfully, then it means the deployed virtual machine is ready with an installed runtime environment.

7. Go to the **PetClinic-CloudProvisioning** job and select **Build other projects** from **Add Post-build Actions**.

8. Enter **PetClinic-Deploy** in **Projects to build**:

9. Once the artifact copy operation has verified, configure the build job so we can deploy it as a manual operation. We will create a job with the **String Parameter** of a newly created instance's domain name or IP address:

10. Configure the build job to execute deployment of a WAR file in an AWS instance by executing the following commands:

```
ssh -i /home/mitesh/book.pem -o
StrictHostKeyChecking=no -t -t ec2-user@$AWSDNS
"sudousermod -a -G tomcat ec2-user; sudochmod -R
g+w /var/lib/tomcat6/webapps; sudo service tomcat6
stop;"

scp -i /home/mitesh/book.pem
/home/mitesh/target/*.war ec2-
user@$AWSDNS:/var/lib/tomcat6/webapps

ssh -i /home/mitesh/book.pem -o
StrictHostKeyChecking=no -t -t ec2-user@$AWSDNS
"sudo service tomcat6 start"
```

11. Execute this command from the **Execute shell** commands section in the Jenkins build job:

12. Once this build job ha executed successfully, it means that the application deployment is successful, so we can perform a functional test.

13. Configure promotion on the **PetClinic-FuncTest** build using the **Promotion** plugin:

14. After execution of **PetClinic-FuncTest**, our pipeline ends:

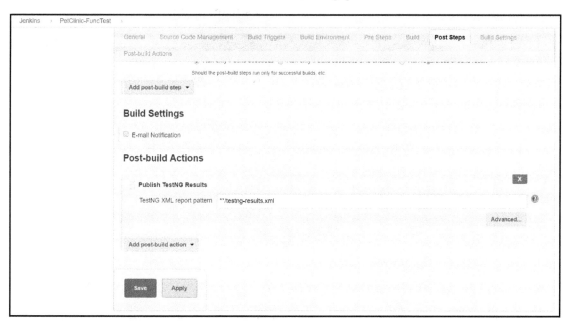

15. Save PetClinic-FuncTest and verify the upstream projects.
16. Install a **Build Pipeline** plugin from **Manage Jenkins** | **Manage Plugins**.
17. On the **Jenkins** Dashboard, click on the **+** sign.
18. Provide a **View name**:

19. **Select Initial Job** in the Upstream / downstream config:

20. Click on **Run** to execute. Make sure that Tomcat and Sonar, which are configured in Jenkins, are running.

21. We have configured **PetClinic-Deploy** as a downstream project in **Build other projects** (manual step). We have defined the parameters too:

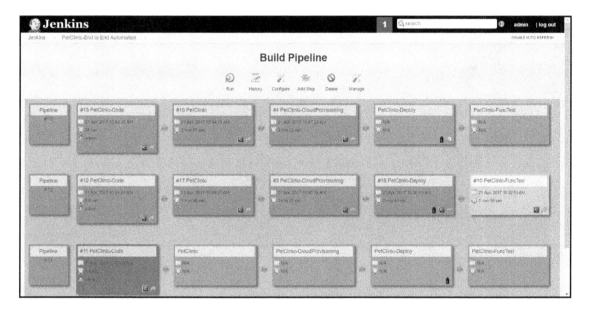

Fig: Build pipeline for end-to-end automation of application life cycle management

22. Verify the parameter symbol:

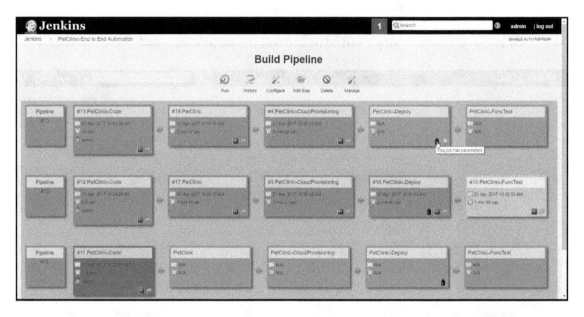

Fig: Build pipeline with parameterized job

23. Once the **PetClinic-CloudProvisioning** project has completed successfully, note the domain name and provide it as a default parameter in the **PetClinic-Deploy** project.

24. Click on **Trigger**:

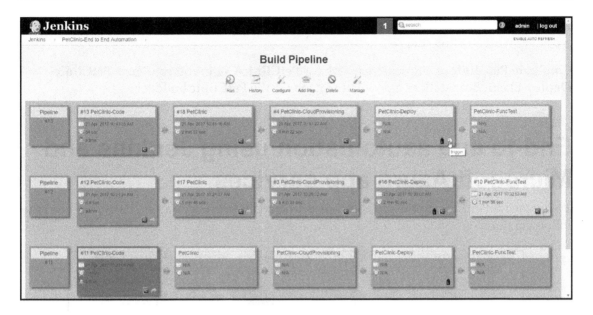

Fig: Build pipeline with manual trigger

25. Verify the end-to-end build pipeline execution.

So, with the use of the **Build Pipeline** plugin we can orchestrate the automation of different activities.

End-to-end automation using Jenkins and AWS Elastic Beanstalk

To deploy the PetClinic Spring application in Amazon Elastic Beanstalk (PaaS), we need the following flow:

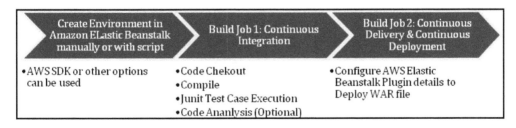

We have **PetClinic-Code**, **PetClinic**, and **PetClinic-Deploy-ElasticBeanstalk** build jobs that we have created in this chapter.

Configure **PetClinic** as a downstream job for **PetClinic-Code**; and configure **PetClinic-Deploy-ElasticBeanstalk** as a downstream job for the **PetClinic** build job.

End-to end aautomation using Jenkins and Microsoft Azure app services

To deploy thePetClinic Spring application in Microsoft Azure web apps (PaaS), we need the following flow:

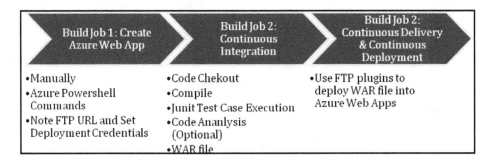

We have **PetClinic-Code**, **PetClinic**, and **PetClinic-Deploy-Azure** build jobs that we have created throughout this chapter. Configure PetClinic as a downstream job for **PetClinic-Code**; and configure **PetClinic-Deploy-Azur**e as a downstream job for the **PetClinic** build job.

In Microsoft Azure's case, there is an alternative as well: we can use the Visual Studio Team server and TFS online for continuous integration, continuous delivery, and continuous deployment.

End-to-end automation orchestration of application life cycle management using VSTS

In Chapter 5, *Continuous Delivery*, we saw how to deploy our web application using VSTS:

1. Go to **Releases** and check the latest release definition.
2. Look at the **Build & Release** column to verify the build number.
3. Double click on **Release-22** to get more details on the release definition execution in VSTS:

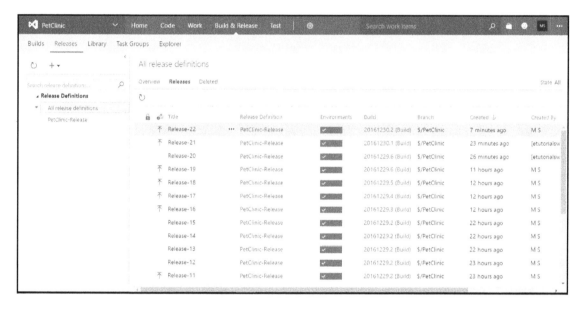

Now let's verify the details we have on the release definition execution in VSTS:

1. In **Details**, verify the build number that triggered the execution of the release definition. It also provides details on the user who requested continuous deployment.

2. The **Environments** section provides details on which the environment release definition has done deployment. It also shows the **Deployment status**: when the release definition was triggered, when it was completed, and whether or not there was any test execution. In our case, there are no test cases in the release definition:

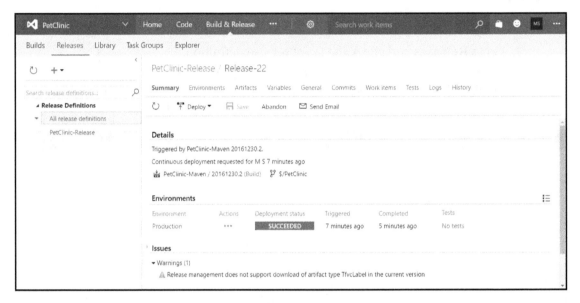

3. To get more details on the release definition execution, click on **Logs**. It will have a series of steps that have been executed during the release definition execution.

4. If the approval mechanism is set, then it will ask for approval first; once approval is given, it will run on an agent. It will initialize the agent first; then, once the agent is available for the release definition execution, it will download the artifact or WAR file from the source folder.

5. We already know that we can't deploy the WAR file directly, so, based on our configuration, it will convert the WAR file into a ZIP file. Once we have a ZIP file of our package, then our Deploy Azure App Service task will deploy the application package into Azure Web Apps.

6. Click on each individual step to get a detailed log on the step execution.

7. Let's see what the **WAR Converter **/*.war** step does.

8. Similarly, the Deploy Azure App Service step execution will give details on how the deployment process is executed:

9. As there is no **Post-deployment** approval configured, it is auto-approved and hence the build execution was successful:

We already know the Azure web application URL, or we can get it from the Azure portal. Visit it and check whether the application has deployed correctly or not.

So, up to this point, we have configured end-to-end automation for application life cycle management using continuous integration and continuous deployment.

We use deployment slots for different environments. So, we should create multiple environments here in the release definition and perform a deployment.

So, the next question should be how to create an environment so we can use it for package deployment in a specific deployment slot in Azure Web Apps?

In the release definition, click on **+Add environment** and select **Create new environment.** We can select **Clone selected environment** if we want to use the same tasks of the existing environment in the new environment:

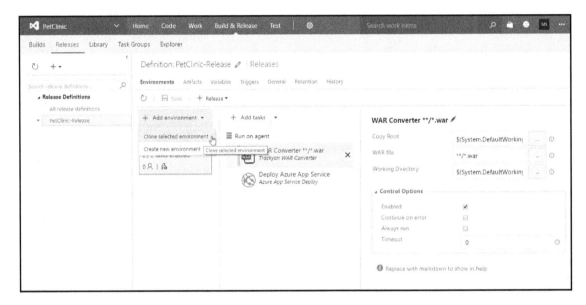

In the new environment, let's keep pre-deployment approval automatic:

1. Select **Trigger** to **Deploy automatically whenever a deployment to the environment Production is successful**. We can rearrange or rename it once all the environments are configured.
2. Select the **Hosted** agent for the release definition execution.
3. Click on **Create**.
4. Change the name of an environment by double-clicking on the **Name of the environment**.
5. Based on the environment, the rest of the deployment details can be configured:

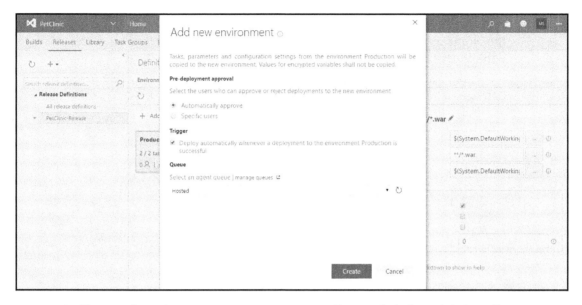

6. Change the existing environment name to **Dev** and click on (**...**). It will open a menu and select the **Clone selected environment** option.

7. In the case of a new environment, what if we want to keep approvals before the deployment process takes place?

8. In the **Pre-deployment approval**, select **Specific users**. All the users available in the VSTS account are eligible for approval rights. We can provide any name from that list.

9. Select **Trigger** to **Deploy automatically whenever a deployment to the environment Dev is successful**. We can rearrange or rename it once all environments are configured.

10. Select the **Hosted** agent for the release definition execution.

11. Click on **Create**. Change the name of an environment as QA by double-clicking on the **Name of the environment**. Based on the environment, the rest of the deployment details can be configured:

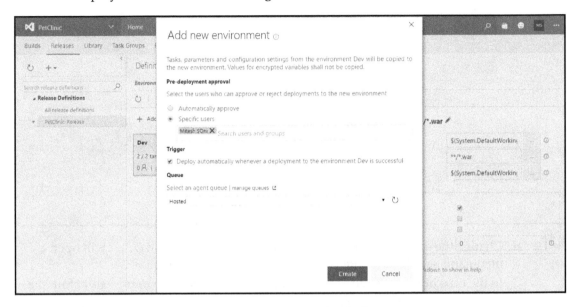

12. Configure the UAT environment in a similar fashion.

13. To assign approvals manually to any environment, select **Environments**, click on (...), and select **Assign approvers...**.

14. In **Pre-deployment approval**, we can specify users who can approve the execution of the release definition for the deployment.

15. Click on **OK**.

16. We need to only configure where to deploy the WAR file in different environments that we have created recently:

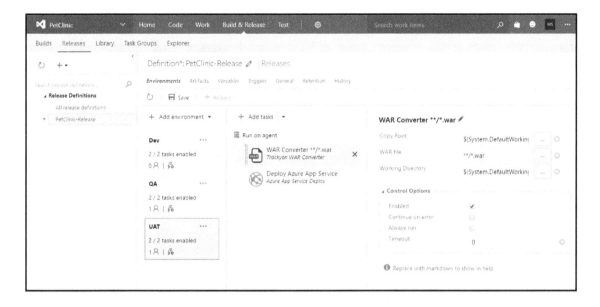

Let's start with the **Dev** environment:

1. Click on the **Dev** environment.
2. Go to **Deploy Azure App Service** task available in the release definition.
3. **AzureRM Subscription** and **App Service Name** are already configured, as we did that exercise earlier
4. To deploy the WAR file into a specific slot, that is **dev** in this case, let's click on the **Deploy to Slot** checkbox.
5. It will ask for the **Resource Group**: select the resource group from which the Azure web application is available.
6. In the **Slot** list, all slots created for the Azure Web Apps will be listed. Select the **dev** slot.

7. Keep the rest of the details as they are and save the release definition:

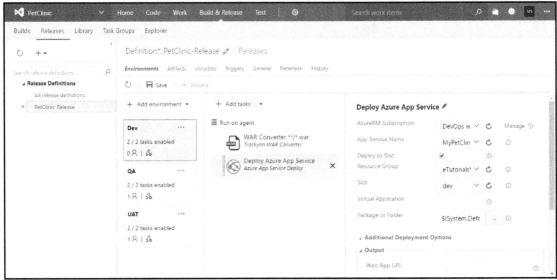

Now, let's configure the **QA** environment:

1. Click on the **QA** environment.
2. Go to the **Deploy Azure App Service** task available in the release definition.
3. **AzureRM Subscription** and **App Service Name** are already configured as we did that exercise earlier too.
4. To deploy the WAR file into a specific slot, that is **qa** in this case, let's click on the **Deploy to Slot** checkbox.
5. It will ask for the **Resource Group**: select the resource group from which the Azure web application is available.
6. In the **Slot** list, all slots created for the Azure Web Apps will be listed. Select the **qa** slot.

7. Keep the rest of the details as they are and save the release definition:

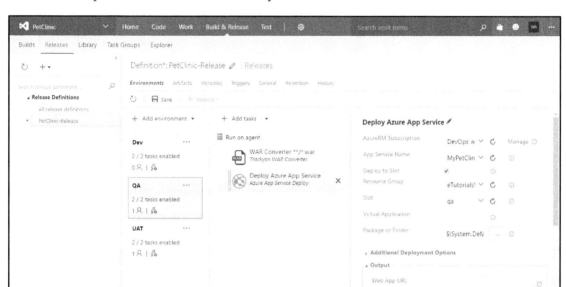

To configure the **UAT** environment, follow these steps:

1. Click on the **UAT** environment.
2. Go to the **Deploy Azure App Service** task available in the release definition.
3. **Azure RM Subscription** and **App Service Name** are already configured, as we did that exercise earlier.
4. To deploy the WAR file into a specific slot, that is dev in this case, let's click on the **Deploy to Slot** checkbox.
5. It will ask for the **Resource Group**: select the resource group in which the Azure Web App is available.
6. In the **Slot** list, all slots created for the Azure Web Apps will be listed. Select the **uat/stage** slot.

7. Keep the rest of the details as they are and save the release definition:

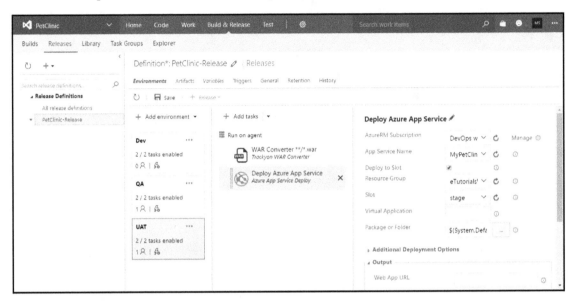

8. To deploy an application in the production slot or main Azure Web Apps, we need not select any slot. We just need to provide the Azure web application name and it will deploy into the main web application in Azure:

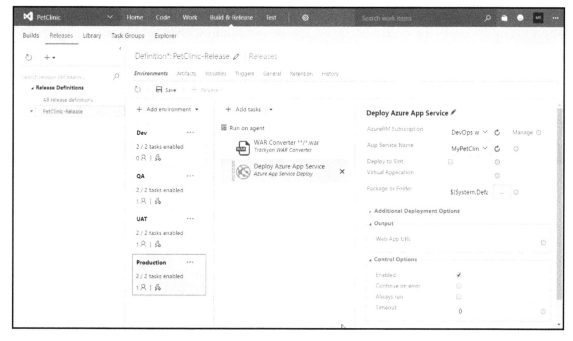

9. Save the release definition:
10. Click on the **Release** link:

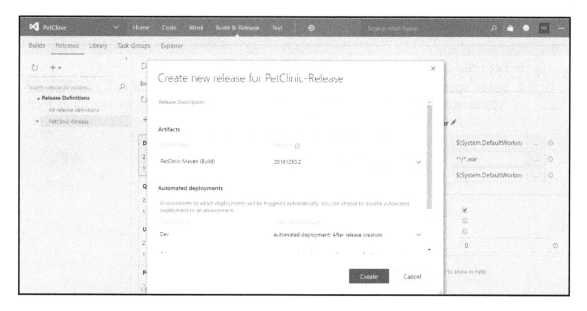

We have set the approval process in the release definition execution so, until and unless the approver approves it, the execution of the release definition won't take place.

Look at the warning available in the summary section of the release definition execution. It says a pre-deployment approval is pending for the `dev` environment.

As I have configured my own ID as the approver, the links are available to approve or reject the build:

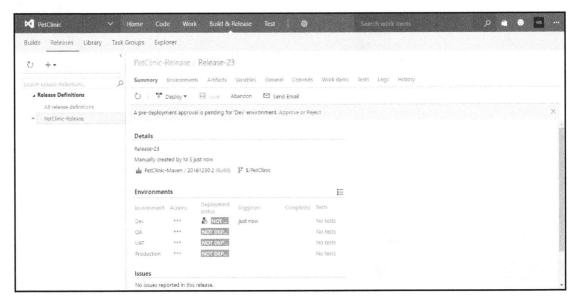

1. Let's click on the **Approve** or **Reject** link.
2. It will open a small dialog box. We need to provide a comment in it and click on **Approve** or **Reject**. We can assign multiple approvers in this mechanism as well, and we can also set whether we want to have approval from either approver, or all approvers.

3. In this case, we will click on **Approve**:

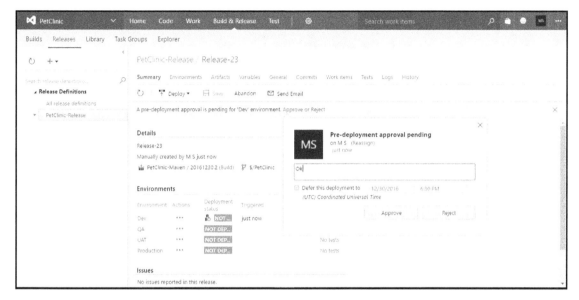

4. In **Logs**, now we can see that **Pre-deployment approval** has been given and the rest of the processes are about to be executed for application deployment in the **Dev** slot:

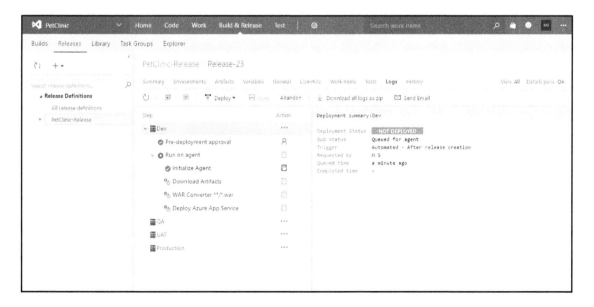

5. The artifact from the build definition will be downloaded so it can be converted to a ZIP file, and then we can deploy it into the **Dev** slot:

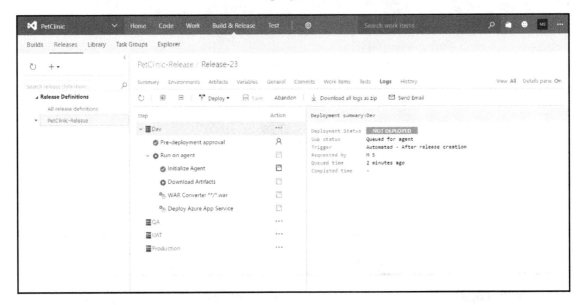

6. Once deployment to the **Dev** environment is successful, the execution process will wait for the approval before it starts deployment into the **QA** slot.

7. We need to provide approval to get the step execution going for the application deployment:

8. In the releases, we can see that there are four different environments, as in our release definition we created those environments.

9. We can see the current status of the release definition execution:

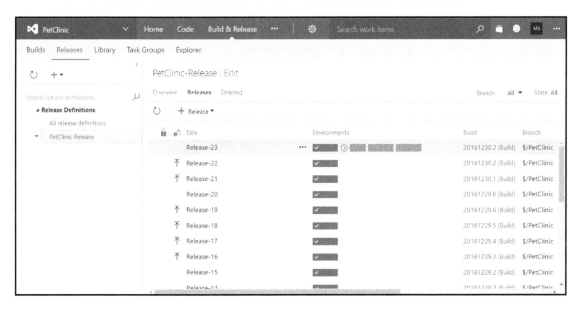

10. Give approvals for the **QA** slot deployment and it will deploy a WAR file into the **QA** slot as well.

We need to remember that the process is going to be the same and nothing is going to change, except some parameters, during the application deployment in the different Azure web application deployment slots.

We need to remember that every slot is a live web application, so if we want to see where the application is deployed and what else is going on behind the scene, then we can go to the Kudu editor for each slot and verify that the operations have taken place for the deployment in each slot of the Azure web application.

Similarly, deploy into the **UAT** or **Stage** slot and **Production** slot too:

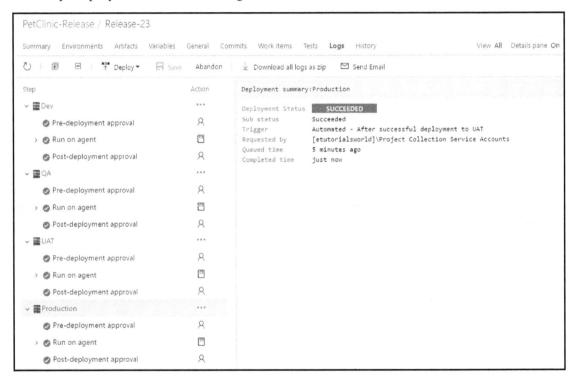

Now, as an exercise on your own, commit some changes in the code of the application and observe how the build definition is executed; how it triggers the release definition after successful execution of the build job; and how an application is deployed on different slots. Once that is done, visit a specific URL of the deployment slot of an Azure web application and check whether the application deployment in different environments has been successful or not.

Summary

In this chapter, we have seen how to automate different tasks that are part of application life cycle management.

We have deployed an application using Jenkins on AWS and Microsoft Azure Cloud service providers. We used the Chef configuration management tool for installing runtime environment.

We also deployed an application on AWS Elastic Beanstalk using Jenkins, and used Visual Studio Team Services for end-to-end automation for deploying the application in Azure App Services, which is a PaaS offering from Microsoft.

In the next chapter, we will learn more about configuring security and monitoring related details. We will look further at role-based access to resources available in Jenkins, VSTS and Microsoft Azure.

8
Security and Monitoring

"Showing a strong success and visible benefits is key to getting others to agree to try your way of doing things.

- Frederic Rivain

Security is one of the most important parts of application life cycle management, hence, this service increases value in the context of DevOps.

In this chapter, we will cover user management, monitoring, and some sections of troubleshooting as well.

We will see how to create users and manage users in both Jenkins and VSTS. With open source and commercial tools, things don't change much in terms of functionality, but they might change with regard to the ease of doing it and extent to which support is available.

We will cover the following topics in this chapter:

- User management in Jenkins
- User management in **Visual Studio Team Services** (**VSTS**)
- Monitoring Jenkins and Microsoft Azure
- Azure Web App troubleshooting and monitoring

Security in Jenkins and VSTS

Security is a major concern with respect to Jenkins and VSTS. However, it is not limited to that aspect only. Security is more about an overall perspective that includes application and infrastructure security. Infrastructure security becomes more crucial considering the fact that we operate in the cloud environment.

In this chapter, we will cover user management in Jenkins and VSTS.

User management in Jenkins

Security is all about **authentication** and **authorization**, which are parts of the AAA trio:

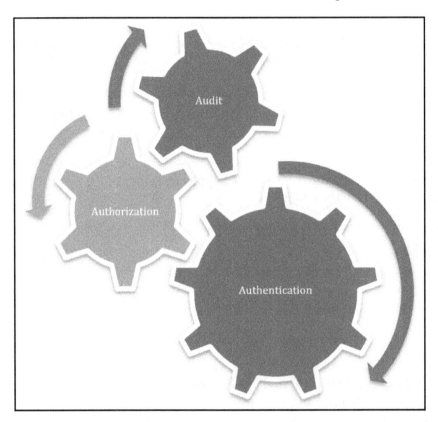

For security configuration, go to **Manage Jenkins** and click on **Configure Global Security** in Jenkins:

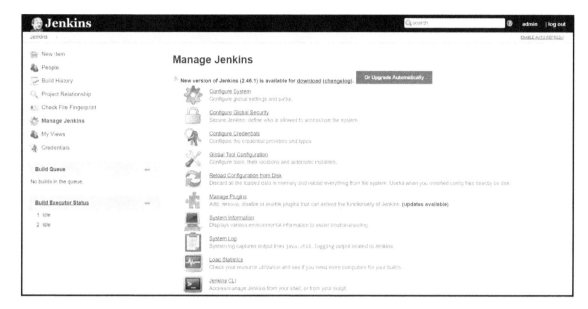

To enable security in Jenkins, click on **Enable Security**. By default, security is enabled in Jenkins:

We need to change **TCP port for JNLPagents** to **Random** so agents can be configured.

For **Access Control** in **Authentication**, select **Jenkins' own user database** in the **Security Realm** section.

Check **Allow users to sign up** so new users can create an account:

In **Authorization**, select **Matrix-based security** to provide rights to all available users as required:

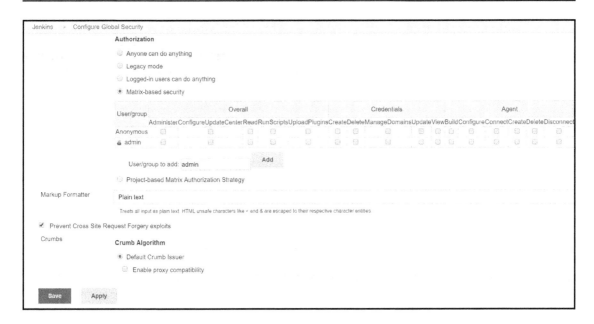

We can also select **Project-based matrix Authorization Strategy**. In this case, we need to go to the individual build job or project and go to its configuration:

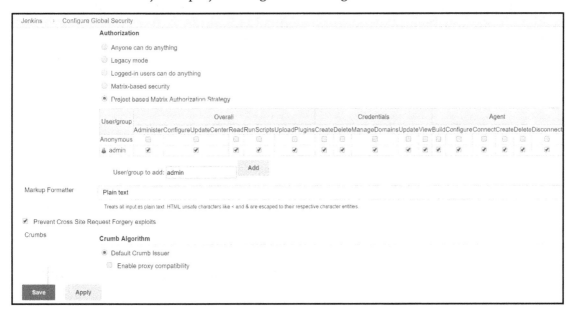

Check **Enable project-based security** and give rights to individual users:

It often happens that we accidently lock our Jenkins by not providing rights to admin users specifically and then saving the security configuration.

In such a scenario, to restore Jenkins access, go to **JENKINS_HOME** in any operating system on which you have installed Jenkins.

Open `Config.xml`, change the value of `useSecurity` to `false` and restart Jenkins:

```xml
<?xml version='1.0' encoding='UTF-8'?>
<hudson>
  <disabledAdministrativeMonitors>
    <string>jenkins.diagnostics.SecurityIsOffMonitor</string>
  </disabledAdministrativeMonitors>
  <version>2.32.1</version>
  <numExecutors>2</numExecutors>
  <mode>NORMAL</mode>
  <useSecurity>true</useSecurity>
  <authorizationStrategy class="hudson.security.ProjectMatrixAuthorizationStrategy">
    <permission>com.cloudbees.plugins.credentials.CredentialsProvider.Create:admin</permission>
    <permission>com.cloudbees.plugins.credentials.CredentialsProvider.Delete:admin</permission>
    <permission>com.cloudbees.plugins.credentials.CredentialsProvider.ManageDomains:admin</permission>
    <permission>com.cloudbees.plugins.credentials.CredentialsProvider.Update:admin</permission>
    <permission>com.cloudbees.plugins.credentials.CredentialsProvider.View:admin</permission>
    <permission>hudson.model.Computer.Build:admin</permission>
    <permission>hudson.model.Computer.Configure:admin</permission>
    <permission>hudson.model.Computer.Connect:admin</permission>
    <permission>hudson.model.Computer.Create:admin</permission>
    <permission>hudson.model.Computer.Delete:admin</permission>
    <permission>hudson.model.Computer.Disconnect:admin</permission>
    <permission>hudson.model.Hudson.Administer:admin</permission>
    <permission>hudson.model.Hudson.ConfigureUpdateCenter:admin</permission>
```

In the next section, we will see user management in VSTS.

User management in VSTS

For configuration and user management, follow these steps:

1. Open the newly created project **PetClinic** and click on the settings icon. On the **Project profile** page, the team information is available. Click on **PetClinic Team**:

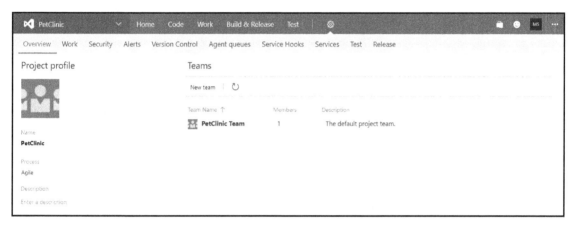

2. By default, the admin account is already available as a team member. Click on **+Add...** to add a new team member for collaboration:

3. Use sign-in addresses or group aliases and click on **Save changes**:

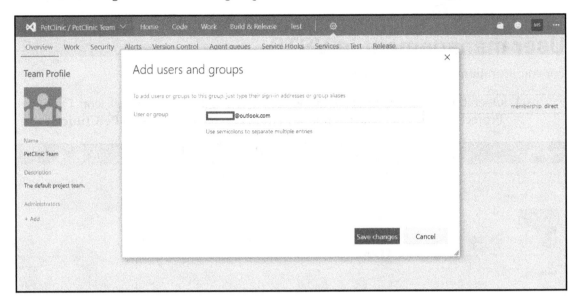

4. Verify the team members of the **PetClinic Team** in the dashboard:

5. Go to the main page of the team project and verify the **Team Members** section as well:

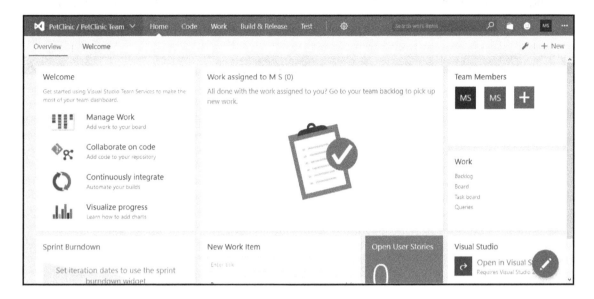

We have successfully added a team member to the main team of the project. This is how we can create a project and manage a team.

Monitoring Jenkins and Microsoft Azure

Azure App Service/Azure Web Apps comes with diagnose and solve problems to find out about resource health and solutions to some common problems.

Monitoring Jenkins

In Jenkins, we can monitor master and different agents with the use of a monitoring plugin:

1. Go to **Manage Jenkins | Manage Plugins** and install **Monitoring Plugins**:

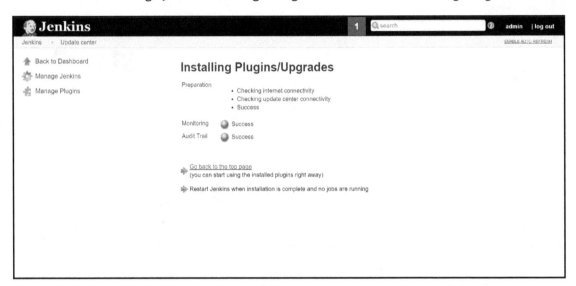

2. After installing it successfully, go to **Manage Jenkins** and select **Monitoring of Jenkins master**.

3. Click on **Jenkins nodes** in the same section to watch monitoring of agents of Jenkins:

Jenkins CLI
Access/manage Jenkins from your shell, or from your script.

Script Console
Executes arbitrary script for administration/trouble-shooting/diagnostics.

Manage Nodes
Add, remove, control and monitor the various nodes that Jenkins runs jobs on.

About Jenkins
See the version and license information.

Manage Old Data
Scrub configuration files to remove remnants from old plugins and earlier versions.

Install as Windows Service
Installs Jenkins as a Windows service to this system, so that Jenkins starts automatically when the machine boots.

Manage Users
Create/delete/modify users that can log in to this Jenkins

Managed files
e.g. settings.xml for maven, central managed scripts, custom files, ...

In-process Script Approval
Allows a Jenkins administrator to review proposed scripts (written e.g. in Groovy) which run inside the Jenkins process and so could bypass security restrictions.

Backup manager
Backup or Restore Jenkins configuration files

Monitoring of Jenkins master
Monitoring of memory, cpu, http requests and more in Jenkins master.
You can also view the monitoring of Jenkins nodes.

Prepare for Shutdown
Stops executing new builds, so that the system can be eventually shut down safely.

4. Verify the statistics of JavaMelody monitoring taken at a specific timestamp in the browser:

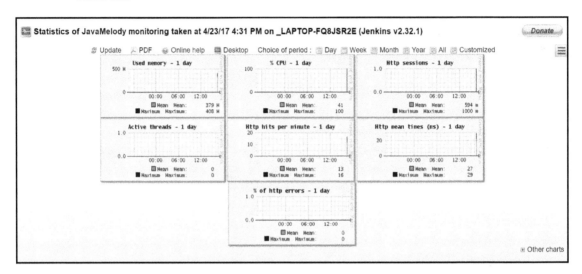

5. Click on **Other charts** to get more information on different aspects of Jenkins, such as buffer memory, threads count, swap space, and so on:

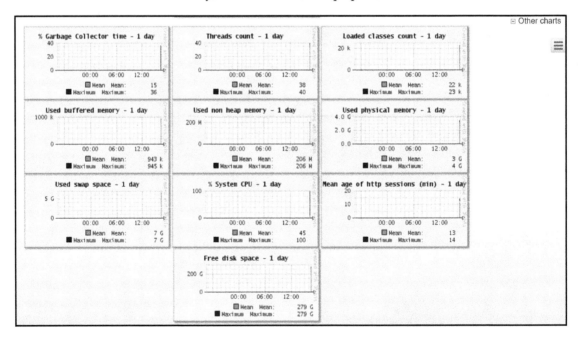

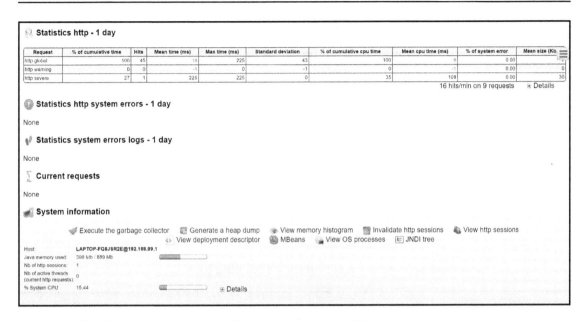

Statistics http - 1 day

Request	% of cumulative time	Hits	Mean time (ms)	Max time (ms)	Standard deviation	% of cumulative cpu time	Mean cpu time (ms)	% of system error	Mean size (Kb
http global	100	45	18	225	43	100	6	0.00	
http warning	0	0	-1	0	-1	0	-1	0.00	0
http severe	27	1	225	225	0	35	109	0.00	30

16 hits/min on 9 requests   ⊞ Details

Statistics http system errors - 1 day

None

Statistics system errors logs - 1 day

None

Current requests

None

System information

Execute the garbage collector   Generate a heap dump   View memory histogram   Invalidate http sessions   View http sessions
View deployment descriptor   MBeans   View OS processes   JNDI tree

Host:	LAPTOP-FQ8JSR2E@192.168.99.1
Java memory used:	398 Mb / 889 Mb
Nb of http sessions:	1
Nb of active threads (current http requests):	0
% System CPU	15.44

⊞ Details

6. Scroll down and get detailed information on **Threads**:

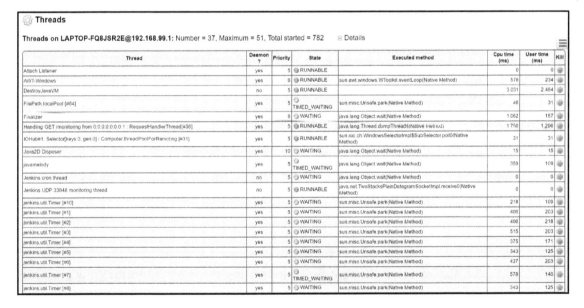

Threads

Threads on **LAPTOP-FQ8JSR2E@192.168.99.1**: Number = 37, Maximum = 51, Total started = 782   ⊟ Details

Thread	Daemon?	Priority	State	Executed method	Cpu time (ms)	User time (ms)	Kill
Attach Listener	yes	5	RUNNABLE		0	0	
AWT-Windows	yes	8	RUNNABLE	sun.awt.windows.WToolkit.eventLoop(Native Method)	578	234	
DestroyJavaVM	no	5	RUNNABLE		3.031	2.484	
FilePath.localPool [#64]	yes	5	TIMED_WAITING	sun.misc.Unsafe.park(Native Method)	46	31	
Finalizer	yes	8	WAITING	java.lang.Object.wait(Native Method)	1.062	187	
Handling GET /monitoring from 0:0:0:0:0:0:0:1 : RequestHandlerThread[#56]	yes	5	RUNNABLE	java.lang.Thread.dumpThreads(Native Method)	1.750	1.296	
IOHub#1. Selector[keys:0, gen:0] / Computer.threadPoolForRemoting [#31]	yes	5	RUNNABLE	sun.nic.ch.WindowsSelectorImpl$SubSelector.poll0(Native Method)	31	31	
Java2D Disposer	yes	10	WAITING	java.lang.Object.wait(Native Method)	15	15	
javamelody	yes	5	TIMED_WAITING	java.lang.Object.wait(Native Method)	359	109	
Jenkins cron thread	no	5	WAITING	java.lang.Object.wait(Native Method)	0	0	
Jenkins UDP 33848 monitoring thread	no	5	RUNNABLE	java.net.TwoStacksPlainDatagramSocketImpl.receive0(Native Method)	0	0	
jenkins.util.Timer [#10]	yes	5	WAITING	sun.misc.Unsafe.park(Native Method)	218	109	
jenkins.util.Timer [#1]	yes	5	WAITING	sun.misc.Unsafe.park(Native Method)	406	203	
jenkins.util.Timer [#2]	yes	5	WAITING	sun.misc.Unsafe.park(Native Method)	406	218	
jenkins.util.Timer [#3]	yes	5	WAITING	sun.misc.Unsafe.park(Native Method)	515	203	
jenkins.util.Timer [#4]	yes	5	WAITING	sun.misc.Unsafe.park(Native Method)	375	171	
jenkins.util.Timer [#5]	yes	5	WAITING	sun.misc.Unsafe.park(Native Method)	343	125	
jenkins.util.Timer [#6]	yes	5	WAITING	sun.misc.Unsafe.park(Native Method)	437	203	
jenkins.util.Timer [#7]	yes	5	TIMED_WAITING	sun.misc.Unsafe.park(Native Method)	578	140	
jenkins.util.Timer [#8]	yes	5	WAITING	sun.misc.Unsafe.park(Native Method)	343	125	

7. Click on **Debugging logs** to get more details:

```
JavaMelody 1.65.0
⊟ Debugging logs

Sun Apr 23 16:29:07 IST 2017    DEBUG    JavaMelody filter init started
Sun Apr 23 16:29:07 IST 2017    DEBUG    OS: Windows 10 , amd64/64
Sun Apr 23 16:29:07 IST 2017    DEBUG    Java: Java(TM) SE Runtime Environment, 1.8.0_111-b14
Sun Apr 23 16:29:07 IST 2017    DEBUG    Server: jetty/9.2.z-SNAPSHOT
Sun Apr 23 16:29:07 IST 2017    DEBUG    Webapp context:
Sun Apr 23 16:29:07 IST 2017    DEBUG    JavaMelody version: 1.65.0
Sun Apr 23 16:29:07 IST 2017    DEBUG    JavaMelody classes loaded from: file:/C:/Users/Mitesh/.jenkins/plugins/monitoring/WEB-INF/lib/javamelody-core-1.65.0.jar
Sun Apr 23 16:29:07 IST 2017    DEBUG    Application type: Jenkins
Sun Apr 23 16:29:07 IST 2017    DEBUG    Host: LAPTOP-FQ8JSR2E@192.168.99.1
Sun Apr 23 16:29:07 IST 2017    DEBUG    parameter defined: storage-directory=/C:\Users\Mitesh\.jenkins\monitoring
Sun Apr 23 16:29:07 IST 2017    DEBUG    parameter defined: http-transform-pattern=/\d+/|/site/.+|/javadoc/.+|/ws/.+|obertura/.+|estReport/.+|iolations/file/.+|/user/.+|/static/\w+/|/adjuncts/\w+/|/bound/[\w\-]+
Sun Apr 23 16:29:07 IST 2017    DEBUG    parameter defined: custom-reports=Jenkins Info,About Monitoring
Sun Apr 23 16:29:07 IST 2017    DEBUG    parameter defined: no-database=true
Sun Apr 23 16:29:07 IST 2017    DEBUG    parameter defined: gzip-compression-disabled=true
Sun Apr 23 16:29:07 IST 2017    DEBUG    parameter defined: system-actions-enabled=true
Sun Apr 23 16:29:07 IST 2017    DEBUG    parameter defined: maven-repositories=C:\Users\Mitesh\.m2\repository,http://repo1.maven.org/maven2,http://repo.jenkins-ci.org/public
Sun Apr 23 16:29:07 IST 2017    DEBUG    log listeners initialized
Sun Apr 23 16:29:07 IST 2017    DEBUG    counters initialized
Sun Apr 23 16:29:07 IST 2017    DEBUG    counters data read from files in C:\Users\Mitesh\.jenkins\monitoring\_LAPTOP-FQ8JSR2E
Sun Apr 23 16:29:08 IST 2017    DEBUG    collect task scheduled every 60s
Sun Apr 23 16:29:13 IST 2017    DEBUG    first collect of data done
Sun Apr 23 16:29:13 IST 2017    DEBUG    JavaMelody filter init done in 6770 ms
Sun Apr 23 16:29:13 IST 2017    DEBUG    counters data read from files in C:\Users\Mitesh\.jenkins\monitoring\nodes
```

8. In the bottom section, we can find the debugging logs:

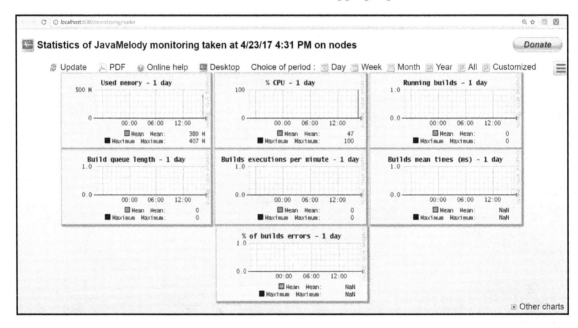

9. We can also monitor different **Build Jobs** using the **Build MonitorView** plugin.

10. Go to **Manage Jenkins | Manage Plugins** and install the **Build Monitor View** plugin:

11. Once it is successfully installed, go to the **Jenkins** dashboard and click on the **+** sign.
12. Provide **View name**.
13. Select **Build Monitor View** and click **OK**:

14. Select the number of jobs you want to monitor.

15. Click on **OK**:

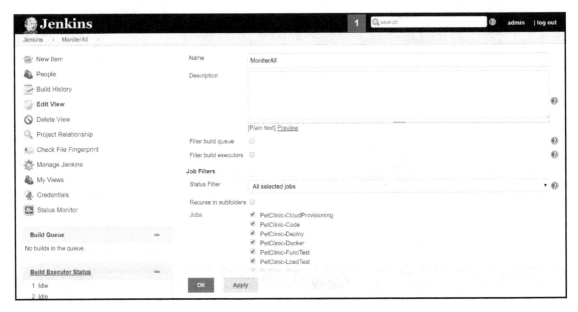

16. From a single window, we can monitor the status of all **Build Jobs** configured in **Build Monitor View**:

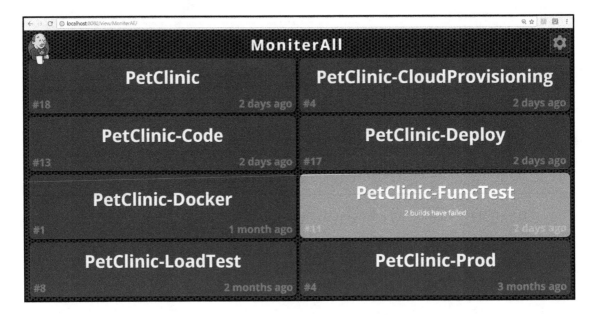

In this book, we have deployed applications on Microsoft Azure Web Apps too, so let's see how to monitor Azure Web Apps and troubleshoot in the next section.

Azure Web Apps troubleshooting and monitoring

Let's deep dive into **Diagnose and solve** problems to get more details:

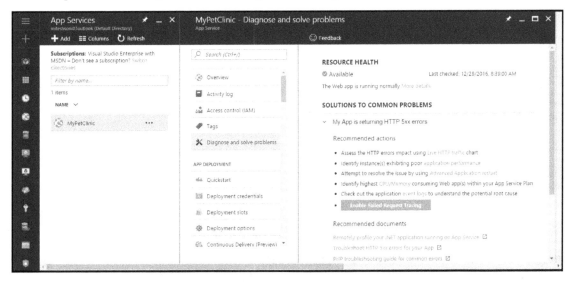

1. Go to Azure **App Services** and select the Azure web application that we created earlier. Click on **Diagnose and solve problems**.
2. Another pane will be opened that will have the **RESOURCE HEALTH** indicator and **SOLUTIONS TO COMMON PROBLEMS**.
3. We can see that the **MyPetClinic** Azure web application is available and running normally based on the status and the green indicator.

In my encounters with Azure Web Apps, I have faced HTTP 5xx errors many times due to various reasons. It is also important to identify the root cause of an issue to fix it. However, there are some quick solution/suggestions given here:

1. In **RESOURCE HEALTH,** click on **More details** to get the existing status of the **MyPetClinic** Azure web application:

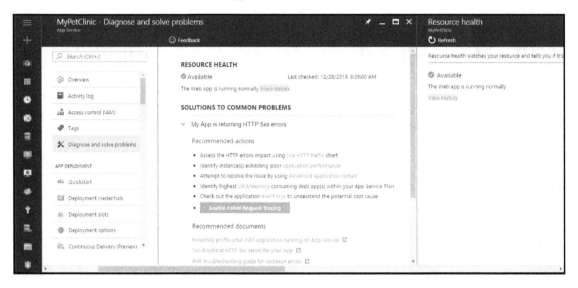

2. Click on **View History** to find details of the Azure web application, regarding when it was available and unavailable:

Azure App Services - HTTP live traffic

In **SOLUTIONS TO COMMON PROBLEMS**, we can assess live traffic to know whether existing resources can manage the current load or not.

If live traffic is normal, then it may not be an issue and we should go a step further to troubleshoot the problem:

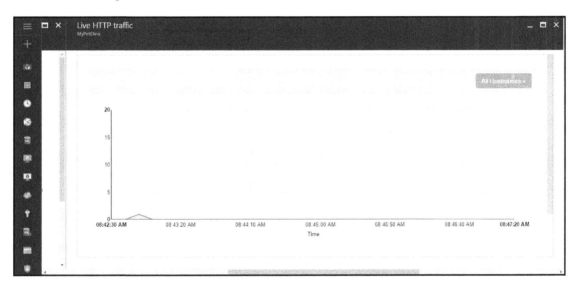

We can get HTTP live traffic based on one or all hostnames available in Azure **App Services**.

Azure App Services - CPU and memory consumption

We can also get details regarding CPU and memory percentage to find the performance of the Azure web application and whether it is required to go for scaling operations:

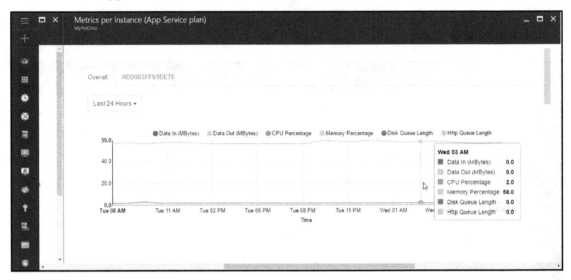

We already know that there is a main Azure web application, and other deployment slots are also available. We can get details of Azure Web Apps or the **Sites In Service Plan** too:

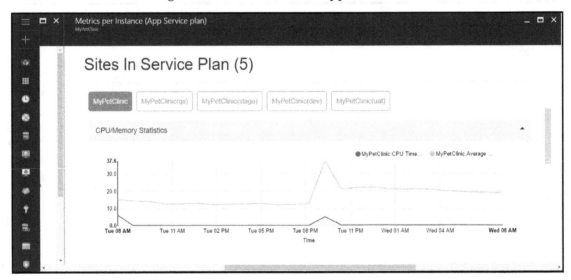

Here, we are looking at the details of the **MyPetClinic(dev)** deployment slot of Azure Web Apps:

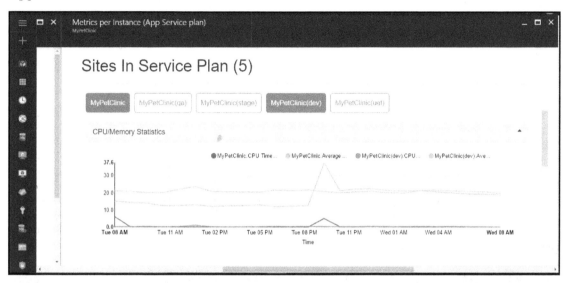

At a time, we can pick and choose the slots or select all of them to see CPU and memory utilization in the **App Service plan** (**ASP**):

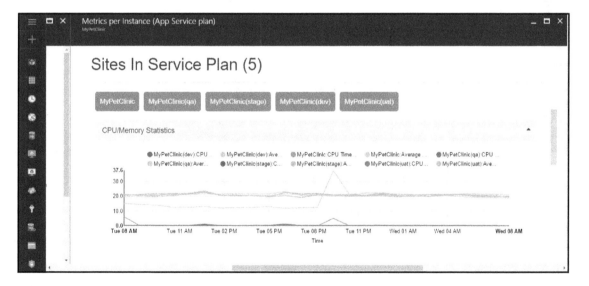

Similarly, we can verify **Http Statistics** for the main Azure web application and deployment slots hosted in a specific ASP:

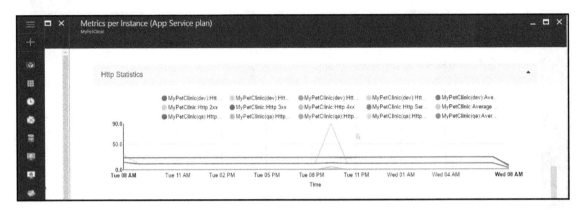

We can also verify **Network Statistics** for the main Azure web application and deployment slots hosted in a specific ASP:

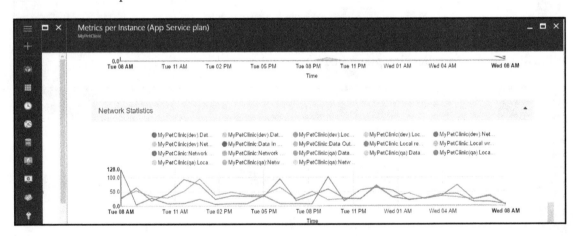

If we keep the cursor on a specific location of the chart, then we will get all the details of that specific point for the main and other deployment slots:

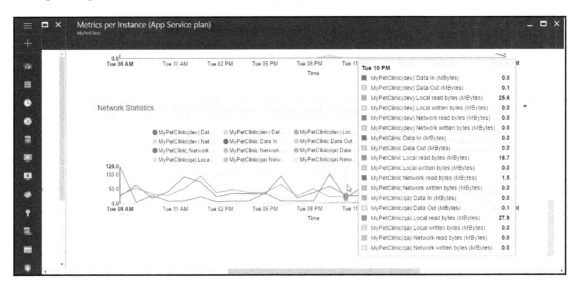

So far, we have seen the diagnose and solve problems section. In the next section, we will look at details related to activity logs.

Azure App Services - Activity log

Activity log shows what actions have been performed in the Azure web application based on **Subscription, Resource group, Resource, Resource type, Operation, Timespan, Event category, Event severity,** and **Event initiated by:**

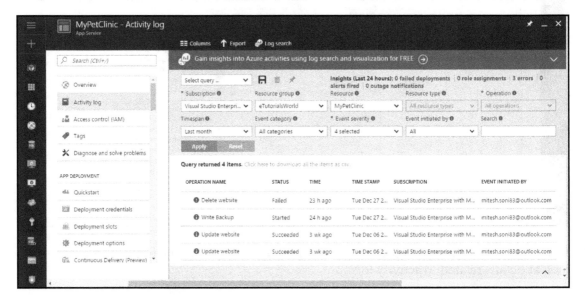

We can see different operations, such as update, write, and delete operations.

Azure Application Insights for application monitoring

In the Azure resource management portal, go to Azure **App Services**, select the Azure web application, and go to the **MONITORING** section; click on **Application Insights**.

Application Insights helps us to identify and diagnose issues in Azure web applications. When we create an Azure web application, we have the option to create **Application Insights** associated with the Azure web application; if we haven't done it, then we can create a new Application Insights resource too for our Azure web application:

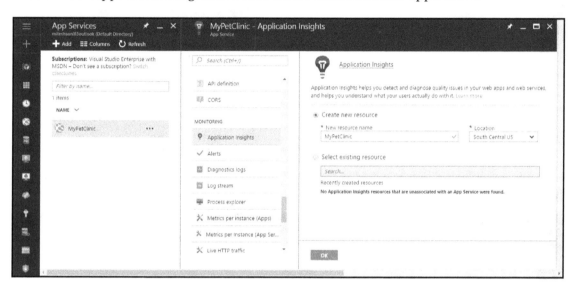

Once the **Application Insights** resource is created, we can access it from the Azure web application also. Let's try to check the availability of the Azure web application from different regions.

In the **INVESTIGATE** tab, click on **Availability**. There is no web test or data available:

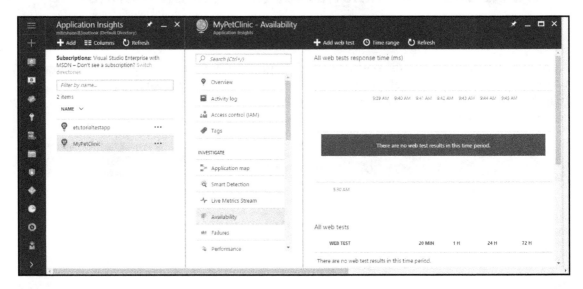

Let's add a web test. Click on **+Add web test**. Provide **Test name**, **URLping test** in **Test type**, and **URL** to test the availability:

In **Test frequency**, select **5 minutes**, and in **Test locations**, select any five locations from where we want to test the availability of an Azure web application:

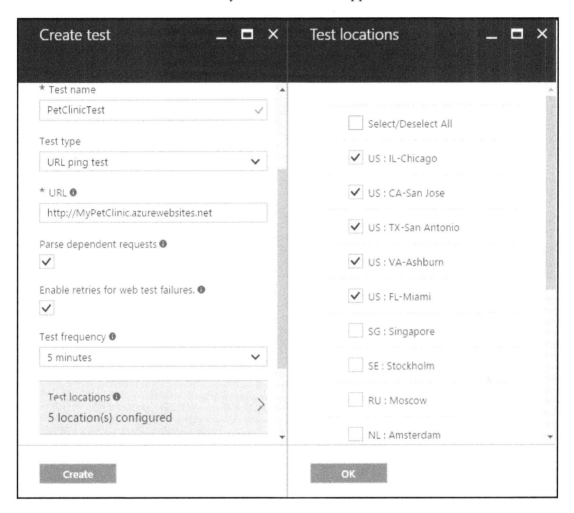

Set **HTTP response: 200** as **Success criteria** and **Alerts** also. After all these configurations, click on **Create**:

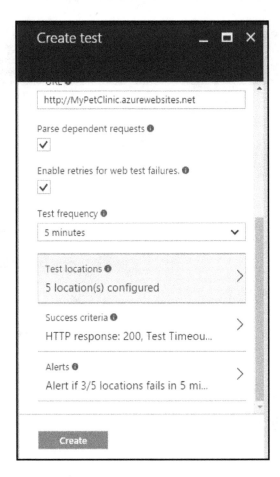

It will start pinging the Azure web application after some time, from the time zone we have configured in the web test. We can see **TOTAL SUCCESSFUL TESTS**, **TOTAL FAILED TESTS**, **AVERAGE RESPONSE TIME**, and other details:

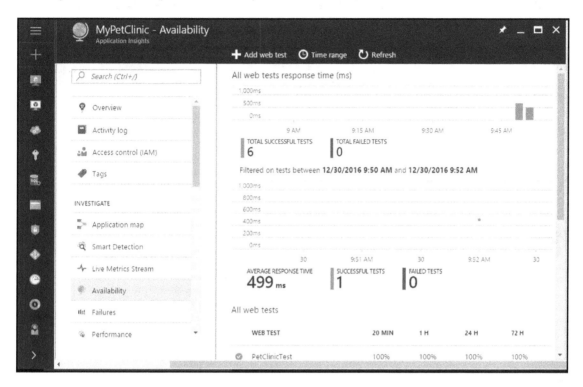

In the **Application Insights** portal, we can see the history of web tests as well.

Azure web application monitoring

We have seen different types of log files in the Kudu editor. Let's see them in the Azure portal.

Diagnostics logs

To enable or disable diagnostics logs, we need to go to Azure **App Services** in the Azure portal, click on the **MyPetClinic** Azure web application, and, in the **MONITORING** section, click on **Diagnostics logs**:

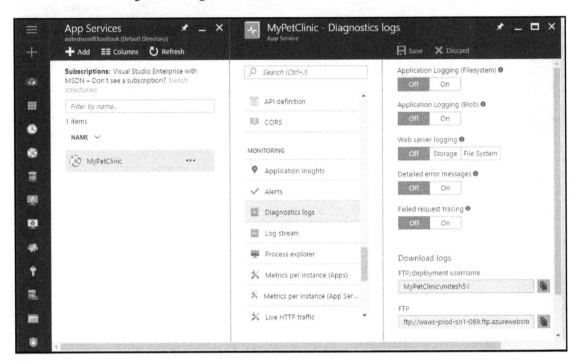

We can enable or disable different kinds of logs based on the need and environment:

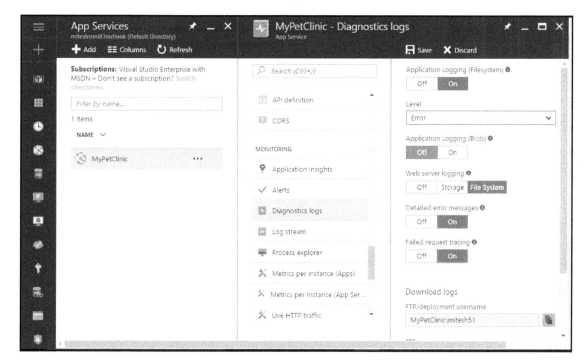

Once changes are done, click on the **Save** button.

Summary

Security and monitoring are concepts that are too vast to be accommodated in one chapter, as they cover different aspects at huge length.

In this chapter, we have covered some aspects of user management and monitoring in Jenkins and VSTS. We have also covered how to diagnose a problem and troubleshoot it in Microsoft Azure App Services or Azure Web Apps.

This is the end of our journey in this book; however, there is no end to education.

The famous quote from Jiddu Krishnamurti says:

> *"There is no end to education. It is not that you read a book, pass an examination, and finish with education. The whole of life, from the moment you are born to the moment you die, is a process of learning"*

Index